The Rise, Spread, and Decline of Brazil's Participatory Budgeting

Brian Wampler • Benjamin Goldfrank

The Rise, Spread, and Decline of Brazil's Participatory Budgeting

The Arc of a Democratic Innovation

palgrave
macmillan

Brian Wampler
School of Public Service
Boise State University
Boise, ID, USA

Benjamin Goldfrank
School of Diplomacy
Seton Hall University
South Orange, NJ, USA

ISBN 978-3-030-90057-1 ISBN 978-3-030-90058-8 (eBook)
https://doi.org/10.1007/978-3-030-90058-8

This Palgrave Macmillan imprint is published by the registered company Springer Nature Switzerland AG.
The registered company address is: Gewerbestrasse 11, 6330 Cham, Switzerland

Acknowledgments

The authors thank Daniel Schugurensky for his excellent review of the full manuscript, Paolo Spada for sharing the latest version of the participatory budgeting in Brazil census, Sheila Holz for her work on the PB census, Wendy Hunter for sharing her database on the Workers' Party, and Mike Touchton for providing data and feedback on the book's argument and scope. We also thank Peter Johannessen for sharing his research on municipal politics with us. In Brazil, we thank Daniel Avelino and Maria do Carmo Albuquerque for discussing these issues via zoom during the pandemic. Over the years, we have greatly benefited from discussing PB-related issues with numerous colleagues within and beyond Brazil. We thank Rebecca Abers, Carla Almeida, Sonia Alvarez, Rocio Annunziata, Leonardo Avritzer, Sérgio Baierle, Gianpaolo Baiocchi, Daniel Chavez, Evelina Dagnino, Luciano Fedozzi, Adrian Gurza Lavalle, Sveinung Legard, Lígia Lüchmann, Luciana Martins da Souza, Stephanie McNulty, Teresa Melgar, Egon Montecinos, Carmen Pineda Nebot, Bill Nylen, Tiago Peixoto, Roberto Pires, Thamy Pogrebinschi, Osmany Porto de Oliveira, Wagner Romão, Matt Ryan, David Sasaki, Aaron Schneider, Paolo Spada, Luciana Tatagiba, Ana Claudia Teixeira, and Yanina Welp. We benefited from the work of several student researchers at Seton Hall University and Boise State University: Elizabeth Theodore, Chevon Erasmus, and Emily Pape. We also thank William Arhip-Paterson, Guillaume Petit, and Giles Pradeau for inviting us to present an early version of the book project at a conference they organized: "Participatory Budgeting in 2020: Participation Without Democracy?" Finally, we thank several colleagues who offered suggestions on earlier versions of some of the arguments made here: Carla

Bezerra, Yves Cabannes, and Françoise Montambeault. Brian Wampler thanks Boise State University and its School of Public Service for providing research support for this book project. Ben Goldfrank thanks Seton Hall University for the University Research Council summer grant that supported his initial work on this project.

Contents

Acronyms

CGU	Comptroller General of the Union (Brazil)
CSO	Civil Society Organization
FASE	Federation of Social Assistance and Education Organizations
FGV	Getúlio Vargas Foundation
FNPP	National Forum for Popular Participation
IBASE	Brazilian Institute for Social and Economic Analysis
INESC	The Institute for Socio-economic Studies
NGO	Non-governmental organization
OECD	Organization for Economic Co-operation and Development
OIDP	International Observatory on Participatory Democracy
OP	*Orçamento Participativo*
PC do B	Communist Party of Brazil
PMDB	Brazilian Democratic Movement Party
PB	Participatory Budgeting
PBP	Participatory Budgeting Project
PP	People Powered
PSB	Brazilian Socialist Party
PSDB	Brazilian Social Democratic Party
PT	Workers' Party
RBOP	Brazilian Network of Participatory Budgeting

List of Figures

List of Tables

CHAPTER 1

Introduction

Abstract During Brazil's transition to democracy during the 1980s and early 1990s, municipal governments and civil society activists created an innovative democratic institution, Participatory Budgeting (PB), that incorporated citizens into public deliberative forums in which participants voted for infrastructure projects. By 2020, PB was one of world's most widely adopted participatory programs, but it has largely been abandoned in Brazil, the country where it all began. This book seeks to explain this puzzling transformation by accounting for the broader arc of PB's creation, spread, and decline in Brazil. We start by asking, what explains why one of the most unequal countries in the world (Brazil) widely adopted an innovative participatory institution? We then ask, why did PB spread across Brazil? What explains why a wide range of Brazilian municipal governments would adopt this particular type of program? But we also seek to explain the slow decline of PB use in Brazil. Why are so few governments using it now? Why is it no longer a vibrant democratic space? What explains the failure of PB to consolidate in Brazil? And what might PB's arc in Brazil tell us about its potential future in other countries?

Keywords Participatory budgeting • Brazil • Democratic innovation • Diffusion • Decline

B. Wampler, B. Goldfrank, *The Rise, Spread, and Decline of Brazil's Participatory Budgeting*,
https://doi.org/10.1007/978-3-030-90058-8_1

During Brazil's transition to democracy during the 1980s and early 1990s, municipal governments and civil society activists created an innovative democratic institution that incorporated citizens into public deliberative forums in which participants ranked infrastructure projects in order of importance. Governments subsequently implemented the selected projects in the participants' communities, often in poor communities, marking a radical change in how governments decide which public projects should be implemented and where. The program, known as Participatory Budgeting (PB, or *Orçamento Participativo* in Portuguese), quickly spread across Brazil and then traveled across the rest of the world (Dias, 2018). In the last decade of the twentieth century and the first decade of the twenty-first century, Brazil became a model of participatory democracy for activists and scholars (Avritzer, 2002; Cameron et al., 2012; Fung, 2011; Fung & Wright, 2003; Pogrebinschi & Samuels, 2014; Sandbrook, 2014; Santos, 2005). Political activists, policy experts, government officials, and academics from across the globe traveled to Brazil, mostly to the city of Porto Alegre, to learn about this participatory institution that appeared to be empowering citizens and improving the provision of public goods and services (Peck & Theodore, 2015; Porto de Oliveira, 2017).

And yet, as PB continues to spread across the globe today, it has largely been abandoned in Brazil, the country where it all began. This book seeks to explain this puzzling transformation by accounting for the broader arc of PB's creation, spread, and decline in Brazil. We start by asking, what explains why one of the most unequal countries in the world (Brazil) widely adopted an innovative participatory institution? We then ask, why did PB spread across Brazil? What explains why a wide range of Brazilian municipal governments would adopt this particular type of program? But we also seek to explain the slow decline of PB use in Brazil. Why are so few governments using it now? Why is it no longer a vibrant democratic space? What explains the failure of PB to consolidate in Brazil? And what might PB's arc in Brazil tell us about its potential future in other countries?

The Arc: 1988–2020

PB's roots developed gradually in several municipalities during the 1980s, when Brazil was transitioning to democracy (Abers, 1996; Pignaton, 2005; Tranjan, 2016). It was formally branded as*orçamento participativo* (participatory budgeting) in Porto Alegre in 1989 and adopted by at least 11 other cities by 1992 (Abers, 1996, 2000; Santos, 1998; Torres Ribeiro

& Grazia, 2003). From 1992 to 2004, the number of municipalities adopting or re-adopting PB grew from 12 to 138, including 17 state capitals.[1] However, just as PB was taking off outside Brazil, spreading to 11,000 programs in over 40 countries worldwide (Dias, 2018; Porto de Oliveira, 2017; Wampler et al., 2021), the number of cities using PB within Brazil began to decline, falling to 126 in 2008 and eventually to fewer than 50 in 2020.[2] This local reversal of fortune for a well-known international "best practice" is especially intriguing because the decline began shortly after the arrival to Brazil's Presidency for the political party most associated with PB, the Workers' Party (*Partido dos Trabalhadores*, or PT). See Fig. 1.1, below, to better visualize the rise, spread, and decline of PB in Brazil.

Explaining PB's trajectory in Brazil requires conceptualizing PB as a political institution; it is not merely a neutral, technical tool of good governance, nor is it a normatively driven democratic cure-all (Baiocchi & Ganuza, 2017; Cabannes & Lipietz, 2017; Dias, 2018). The adoption of new democratic institutions is an intensely political process because of the possibility of altering the distribution of power, resources, and rights (Goldfrank, 2011; McNulty, 2011; Wampler, 2007). Democratic institutions' "emancipatory" potential (Baiocchi & Ganuza, 2017), their capacity to empower politically marginalized groups and their potential to reorient state resources to poor, marginalized communities, can alter the traditional balance of power. Elected officials and their civil society allies are motivated to adopt these institutions to build a base of support as well as to promote longer-term projects, while their rivals may wish to modify, obstruct, or reject any new institutions that might put them at a disadvantage. Thus, it is vital to foreground our analysis with the understanding that—in addition to or even instead of purely "good government" goals—the adoption of new democratic institutions is often politically motivated.

[1] In this chapter, when we refer to the number of cases of PB in Brazilian municipalities, we are referring to those cities with over 50,000 residents, which come to roughly 580 municipalities, or a tenth of all Brazilian municipalities, where between 70 and 80% of Brazil's total population resided from the 1990s to the 2020. The data on PB comes from Wampler and Avritzer (2005), Spada (2020), and updates by the authors.

[2] The Brazilian Institute for Geography and Statistics reported use of budget councils in 2001 (finding 271) and later PB commissions or committees in 2014 (finding 47) for all municipalities; comparing the figures indicates a sharp decline of PB in all cities, large and small (IBGE, 2001, 2014).

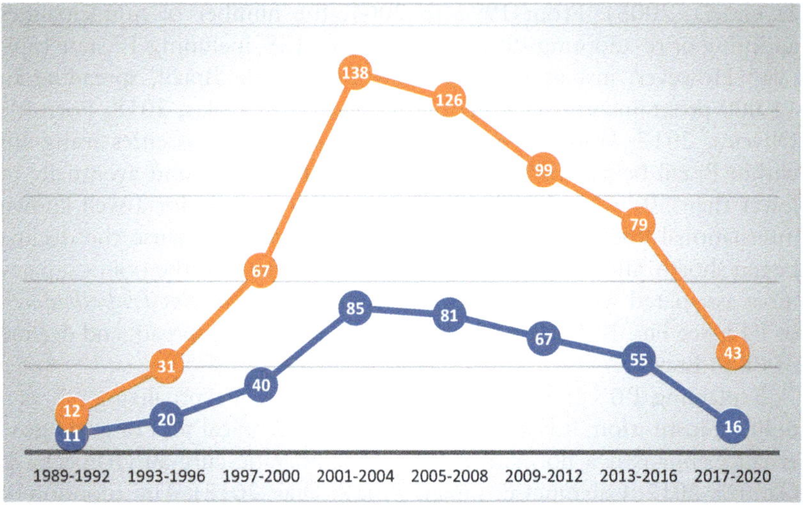

Fig. 1.1 Rise and decline of PB. Orange is all PB cases; Blue is all Workers' Party & other leftist parties' cases

As Fig. 1.1 demonstrates, PB began in the early 1990s in 12 municipalities and reached its height, in terms of the numbers of municipal adoptions, in 2004. Just as the Workers' Party, Brazil's principal proponent of PB, was beginning a 14-year hold on the presidency (2003–2016), this democratic innovation began to decline. In this book, we explain PB's broad arc over a 30-year period, contributing to empirical, methodological, and theoretical debates. We draw from institutional, political choice and civil society literatures to generate theory that accounts for the creation, spread, and decline of an innovative democratic institution. This theory-building process more narrowly focuses on PB, but our broader argument may also be applicable to other democratic innovations.

Argument

To explain the arc of PB adoption in Brazil, we argue that a shifting incentive structure for political parties, civil society organizations (CSOs), and citizens to support and adopt PB changed over a 30-year period. We identify three distinct moments corresponding to different incentive structures: Creation, Spread, and Decline. This book draws from multiple theoretical debates and analytical approaches to provide a more comprehensive understanding of the broader lifecycle of this democratic innovation; PB is located at the interface of communities, civil society, elected governments, and local states, which means that a comprehensive accounting of the creation, spread, and decline requires that we simultaneously consider these processes from multiple perspectives. In Chap. 2, we develop a multi-level analytical framework, inspired by the work of Giraudy et al. (2019), that includes internal (within municipality), horizontal, and vertical factors that explain why municipalities adopted PB. Throughout this book, we demonstrate how this multi-tiered approach provides the most comprehensive explanation regarding why governments decide to adopt or not to adopt PB. Nonetheless, it is important to emphasize one specific political party as particularly relevant in each of the three moments: the Workers' Party.

The Workers' Party is a distinctive political party not just in Brazil but also across the world because of its ability to incorporate social movements, labor unions, community organizations, and the progressive middle class into the governing coalition (Keck, 1992; Hunter, 2010). This was the party at the helm of the municipal government that helped co-create and consolidate PB's institutional design in Porto Alegre and the party that led the effort to spread PB across Brazil. In fact, the Workers' Party was responsible for the adoption of well over half of all PB programs (see Fig. 1.1, above); it sought to show how PB helped local governments "invert" access to political power and resources by incorporating poor citizens into formal spaces. Later on, however, after the Workers' Party reached the presidency, it ended efforts to promote PB, eventually becoming no more likely than other parties to adopt PB. We briefly describe these moments below, and we develop the arguments more completely in subsequent chapters. Chapter 3 analyzes PB's creation, Chap. 4 analyzes the spread of PB across Brazil, and Chap. 6 analyzes PB's decline.

First, the creation of PB's innovative institutional design (combining mass mobilization and incremental policymaking) took place during a critical juncture—Brazil's democratization led to extensive experimentation within civil society and by municipal governments as they sought to expand how, when, and where citizens could exercise voice, vote, and oversight. The long, drawn-out redemocratization movement was conterminous with decentralization (Goldfrank, 2011) and with the expansion of civil society (Alvarez, 1990; Avritzer, 2002; Dagnino, 1994, 1998). Because the goals of many civil society activists aligned with those of the

Workers' Party, when the party won municipal elections, moments of collaborative experimentation emerged. In other words, the long redemocratization allowed an emergent civil society to punctuate Brazil's political equilibrium, thus opening the opportunity for new institutions, practices, and actors to develop. And once the equilibrium was punctuated, a critical juncture around inclusionary democratic institutions was established. Brazil built an extensive participatory architecture that extends far beyond PB, including the establishment of more than 50,000 policy councils by 2010 (Santos Barreto, 2011; Wampler, 2015). We explore this topic in much greater detail in Chap. 3, PB's creation, where we examine the initial conditions and the incentive structures that encouraged government officials and civil society activists to adopt PB.

Second, as Brazil's economy, federal structure, party system, and civil society consolidated during the 1990s and 2000s, we argue that a clear set of political incentives led more and more municipal governments to adopt PB. Specifically, PB spread because some mayors believed that it would improve governance and give them a comparative advantage at the ballot box. During PB's "spread," the need to create new institutions decreased, and there was a greater focus on adopting programs that appeared to be working. As we explain in Chaps. 3 and 4, the Workers' Party was actively involved in promoting PB throughout Brazil. We draw from debates on diffusion, party systems, and elite signaling to explain why governments would adopt PB. Parallel to the adoption of PB was the voluntary adoption of public policy councils, but the key difference is that PB was not generally codified into law whereas the policy councils were.

Third, the adoption of PB reached its numeric peak in 2004 (138 cases), and the number of PB adoptions slowly declined from the mid-2000s through 2020, when there were roughly 40 cases, many of which were quite limited in nature. During this third moment, there were limited political and policy incentives that led government officials to adopt PB. The Workers' Party, the principal political party affiliated with PB, won four consecutive presidential elections (2002, 2006, 2010, 2014), which appeared to cement its control at the federal level. The Workers' Party began to withdraw its support from PB, preferring to use its influence at the federal level in other ways. Moreover, mayors in general stopped adopting PB because of recentralization in the 2000s, the lack of electoral pay-offs from PB, and, for some, because PB was associated with the Workers' Party brand, which became tarnished by corruption scandals. Thus, by 2012, the three political parties (PT, PSDB, and PMDB) that account for most PB adoption largely discontinued their support. Furthermore, most of the 43 cases remaining in 2020 were what we are labeling as "restricted" programs, which means that these PB programs were mostly empty shells.

What Is Participatory Budgeting, and How Did It Work in Porto Alegre?

You may hear the word budget and feel your eyes immediately glaze over, but bear with us. Millions of people in Brazil and now worldwide have participated in PB. While we were in Porto Alegre for the first time, 25 years ago, the city government received official visitors from France, Canada, Argentina, Senegal, and the World Bank, all trying to learn about PB.

As practiced in Porto Alegre from 1989 to the early 2000s, PB allowed average citizens the opportunity to make decisions about local government spending. In a series of public assemblies, participants discussed and debated spending priorities and then voted on which local services were the most important for their neighborhood and city district. Does our neighborhood need sewage lines installed, roads paved, a family health clinic, all of the above? Or do we need a neighborhood library or a new soccer field? Which of all these things should come first? These issues were discussed in two rounds of assemblies at different community levels.

The first round took place at the neighborhood level.[3] This is where people made the real decisions about their priorities. The voting from the neighborhoods was aggregated up to the district level. Then, delegates selected by the participants took a final vote on the priorities for the district. The second-round meetings were districtwide. There, the participants evaluated how well the government complied with the previous year's budget. Neighbors could give their opinions directly and publicly to the mayor and his cabinet members. They also presented the administration with their budget proposal and elected representatives to serve on a citywide budget council and to coordinate a district budget forum.

After the priorities were decided, the city administration used the vote tallies from the districts to determine where and on which projects or

[3] For a detailed account of PB's rules and procedures, see "A Guide to Participatory Budgeting" (Wampler, 2000). This guide was originally published on behalf of the Ford Foundation as part of their Innovations in Good Government program.

services to spend the most money. The way the administration allocated spending is interesting because it used three transparent criteria that the PB participants decided on. Therefore, everyone, or at least everyone who participates, knew the criteria that determined government spending, and participants re-debated the criteria each year. The first and most heavily weighted criterion was—what public service does the community prioritize as most important? Second was how needy the district is in terms of the particular service. For example, what percentage of homes in the district had running water? Last was the size of the district—the larger the population, the more investment it received. Using these three criteria, the government created an annual investment plan and distributed the plan to the participants in the assemblies. The participants, in turn, monitored the implementation of the plan to ensure that their decisions were respected.

Those components are the core of the PB: public decision-making, transparent criteria for government spending, and public oversight. Participatory budgeting is not a one-shot policy event; these components continue throughout the year and they are carried over into the following year's budgetary cycle. The district forums and city budget council continued to meet to debate the finer points of the budget and to discuss city services in general with administration officials. At the end of each year, they also discussed the PB's rules with the administration and made changes to rules they opposed. Often the changes were minor, but some big changes have occurred. In 1994, for example, they created five thematic forums to supplement the district forums, including one for transportation, one for health and social services, and one for education, culture, and sports.

The meetings held by the district and thematic forums and the city budget council were always open to the public. When we went to the meetings, there were always lots of people who either just wanted to learn about how it worked, or who had a question or complaint for city officials. They would say: "Why hasn't the school in my district been built yet? It was in last year's budget plan, what's going on?" Or: "The contractors paving the street in my neighborhood are cheating—They're using only 2 inches of asphalt, not 5. This project is coming from the taxes I paid and I want it done right!" These meetings were not always harmonious.

Prior to the invention of PB, city officials made decisions about spending behind closed doors. Some public works projects were initiated in poor neighborhoods, but these projects were often granted either through *amiguismo* (personal favors for friends) or as political favors in exchange for votes. This point was reiterated to us in dozens of interviews. One favorite story about personal favors was told by a city chauffer who was about 70 years old and still worked driving officials around town. This chauffer, call him Jorge, had great information on corruption scams that took place especially during the period of military rule (1964–1985). The example here was how he decided which house to buy. Jorge had been saving money, he had just got married, and he was choosing among three houses. But they were all far from downtown and all were located on unpaved streets. So Jorge showed his boss, the engineer in charge of street paving, a map showing three streets where his potential houses were. He asked which street was most likely to be paved first. His boss said, "According to logic, it should be this one, because it's closest to the center of town." Before Jorge could argue, because he really liked a house on another street, his boss said "Why?" Jorge told him he had a choice of three houses and wanted to get the one on the street that would be paved soonest. His boss said, "Don't worry, pick the one you like best. We'll pave its street first." Jorge bought a house in August; the street was paved by November.

In general, though, before PB, most city investments were made in large, visible projects in the center of town, like bridges and tunnels, and not in hidden projects like sewage lines or paved streets for the poor, outlying areas of the city. Before 1989, less than half of local residents lived in houses connected to sewage lines. Most streets in the poor areas were unpaved. Hundreds of thousands of residents had thus lived for years in neighborhoods with open-air sewers and unpaved roads. Their streets were often impassable, so they were cut off from essential public services. Police cars, ambulances, and buses would not even enter these poor neighborhoods. In the late 70s and early 80s, community organizations, often united in large networks, protested the lack of services in their neighborhoods. But they received little government response. Politicians made promises to invest in the *favelas* but they only rarely followed through.

When PB first started and offered citizens the chance to say which services they needed, most people thought this was just another political promise that would never deliver. In the first year of PB in Porto Alegre, a city of over a million inhabitants, only about a thousand people came to all the assemblies put together. At first, community organizations were mostly disappointed by PB. They complained that the original structure of participation, with only five districts to hold assemblies, made it hard to organize large groups of people to come. For the next round of assemblies, in agreement with community leaders, government officials further decentralized PB by dividing the city into 16 districts to make participation more manageable. Community leaders also criticized the government's intention to concentrate public works projects in just a few neighborhoods. They argued instead for dispersing projects throughout the city, even if they had to be small. They threatened to boycott PB if it wasn't changed so that each district could benefit. The government yielded to both demands. But the biggest disappointment for activists came in the next year, when the government failed to deliver on hardly any of the projects promised in the budget.

Participation in that year's assemblies declined even compared to the first year's low turn-out. The big problem was that the previous city government had left the coffers empty. The prior mayor gave city workers a large raise at the end of his term, so that the next administration would have to pay for it. However, toward the end of 1990, the administration's financial situation began to change for two reasons. First, federal government revenue transfers began to increase because of decentralizing changes made in the 1988 Constitution. Second, the new mayor redid the city's tax structure, making it more progressive and going after tax evaders.

With the city's turn to fiscal health, the administration began to build the public works projects it had promised in the PB assemblies. Our interviewees told us that this was the turning point for PB. When previous participants saw that their decisions really mattered, they went to the next year's meetings to participate again. And as people saw the sewage pipes extended to the neighborhoods near theirs or a new health clinic built, they asked their neighbors: "How did you get that? Oh, it was through PB." After a couple of years of the government investing between 10 and 20% of its budget on projects like these, more and more neighbors began to participate.

Participatory budgeting turned out to be an excellent tool for mobilizing people to become interested in civic life. A classic example of someone who got involved in public affairs because of PB is "Zeca"—a city budget councilor interviewed in 1999. Asked why he started participating in PB, Zeca said:

> It was to get projects for my neighborhood. The first one was a big project to get drainage pipes installed to stop the flooding on the streets that happened every year in the rainy season. People had complained about it for

> twenty-four years and nothing was ever done. Even though I'd lived there for years, I never really was interested. But after some point I got interested because I saw that no one else was solving the problem, and I had always thought, why should I go if there are other people who can do it? But a couple of years ago I realized that other people weren't doing anything either, so I started going directly to the city cabinet offices and asking for this project. But they wouldn't help me, they always said, no, you have to go to the PB. So I went to a budget meeting and they asked me, what neighborhood association are you from? Because to really get anything done you have to be with a group of people, you can't just go by yourself. I had never been to the association in my neighborhood. When I found it, the president of the association was completely without any ideals, he wasn't doing anything, he didn't even hold meetings. So I proposed holding a new election of the association and with a few other people we made a slate of candidates and we won. Then we went back to the PB with a big group of people from the association and we got our project to be the number one priority in the district. That was last year, and now it's being built.

In addition to encouraging participation in neighborhood and city public affairs, PB led to a transformation of urban infrastructure in dozens of neighborhoods, especially in poorer areas (for all figures cited below, see Goldfrank, 2011, 231–237; see also World Bank, 2008). Before PB, less than three-quarters of homes in Porto Alegre were connected to the sewage system. After eight years of PB, that figure was up to 85% of homes. The average amount of street paving went from 4 kilometers a year to 20 kilometers a year. The number of municipally-run schools tripled. The city built nearly 12,000 housing units in 10 years, whereas in the entire 20 years of the military dictatorship (1964–1985) only 9000 units were built. In almost every part of the city we went to do interviews, people would point to a street or a plaza or a soccer field and say, 'we got that through PB.' In many neighborhoods, the interviewees were quite emphatic. In the *Leste* district, for example, "Claudio" reported: "The difference between what Leste was like before and what it is now, in terms of infrastructure, it's a question of the difference between night and day. Not only in pavement, but in health, in education. You know that favela close by here, Vila Pinto? … There were dead dogs, rotting animals in the street, feces running all over the place, in all the streets. There's been a complete change now." Meaningful changes such as these, especially accompanied by and linked to democratic innovations, are relatively rare, which helps explain why both scholars and policy practitioners from around the globe flocked to Brazil to learn about participatory budgeting.

Theoretical Innovations

Indeed, PB programs captured the imagination of scholars and civil society activists, leading them to build new approaches to better conceptualize and theorize about this new process. What made PB distinct? A participatory institution in a highly unequal society as well as in a new democracy; an institution that appeared to be successfully translating citizens' voices into specific policy outcomes; an institution that had specific rules to support equity and social justice, in seeming contrast to the dominant narratives around the neo-liberal downsizing of the state and promotion of market-led strategies; an institution that successfully incorporated poor citizens to deliberate over public resources. There are multiple conceptual and theoretical areas that scholars worked in as they tried to make sense of this new political phenomena, including debates on democracy, civil society, citizenship (*cidadania*), public space, governance, accountability, institutional change, and social justice and equality. We briefly cover these areas to introduce the reader to these theories and concepts.

Boaventura Santos (1998, 2005) identified PB's democratizing potential, arguing that PB had the potential to "democratize democracy" by expanding the breadth of who participates, the location of where decisions are made, and the type of decisions that citizens can make. Santos recognized PB as an effort to move beyond the confines of representative democracy by expanding the *demos*—those who can actively participate in formal public institutions. Rebecca Abers (2000, 220–221) found that a key way in which PB attracted participants and revitalized civic life in Porto Alegre was by focusing on the immediate needs of specific communities. Fung and Wright (2003) developed a model of "Empowered Participatory Governance" (EPG), in which they show how the direct engagement of citizens in public venues has the potential to improve democracy. Their 2003 edited volume offers multiple cases of citizen participation from across the globe, including a chapter by Gianpaolo Baiocchi in which he applies the concept of EPG to the case of Porto Alegre. Baiocchi shows how PB there contributed to "synergizing civil society" by stimulating the growth of community associations.

PB's direct incorporation of citizens also created opportunities for scholars to theorize about the changing role of citizens. Sergio Baierle

(1998) was among the first researchers to highlight how PB was changing the context in which citizens and states negotiated. By focusing on "emergent actors" who are new to formal political institutions, Baierle captured a novel feature about Porto Alegre's PB program: poor and minimally educated individuals were actively involved in a formal, institutionalized political space. This represented an important shift in Brazil, where poor people had never systematically been incorporated to exercise their voice in formal public settings.

Evelina Dagnino's theoretically rich work suggests that this process was helping to expand citizenship rights. Dagnino's broader work asserts that the process of building a new civil society in Brazil during the 1980s and 1990s involved the expansion of the idea of "the right to have rights" (1994 and 1998). Citizens began to see themselves as rights-bearing members of the polity. This was an important shift in people's consciousness because it moved away from being "subjects" in which they thought of themselves as having limited agency to a new position in which citizens were empowered to demand their rights. Baierle's "emergent actors" were infused with Dagnino's idea of greater citizenship rights; these "new actors" carried the new values into PB. Thus, PB becomes a formal institutional practice in which participants can actively exercise their rights.

Avritzer introduced the concept of "Participatory Publics" in his 2002 book to illuminate how citizens were learning to engage in democratic practices within their civil society organizations (see also Wampler & Avritzer, 2004). The core idea is that Brazil's civil society was recreated during the 1980s and 1990s, leading to new types of CSOs as well as more democratic means of working within these organizations. This concept is complementary to the work of Baierle and Dagnino in the sense that these concepts were first seeking to explain a shift within civil society, which was then followed by new ways of acting in formal democratic spaces. This line of research does a particularly nice job of showing how shifts within civil society helped alter citizens' and CSOs' attitudes and behaviors, which prepared them to engage in new democratic environments. In other words, citizens—especially those who had been historically excluded—were then better prepared to engage within new institutions because their participation in civil society had taught them how to deliberate in the public sphere.

The former mayor of Porto Alegre, Tarso Genro, describes PB as a "non-state public sphere" (*espaço público não-estatal*), arguing that PB is a new type of democratic institution, allowing citizens to engage in deliberative decision-making without state domination:

> To construct a non-state public sphere signifies the reversal, the radical reversal, of the process realized under real socialism, in which the state dominated society. It is a civilizing process of the State, a process in which the State becomes a public entity controlled by civil society. (Genro, 1995, 41)

When created, then, PB represented a conscious effort to avoid Soviet-style state control of civil society. Instead, the Workers' Party and many of its CSO allies hoped to build democratic socialism through new state-society interactions.

This theoretically innovative time period first led researchers to engage in deep case studies, often of single cases (Abers, 2000; Baiocchi, 2005; Fedozzi, 1997; Marquetti, 2003). Over time researchers used medium-N and Large-N research designs to explain variation in the quality of the program across multiple cities (Baiocchi et al., 2011; Goldfrank, 2011; Gonçalves, 2014; Montambeault, 2019; Nylen, 2003; Touchton & Wampler, 2014; Wampler, 2007). We turn now to the methodological approach utilized in this book.

Methodological Approach

To account for the creation, spread, and decline of participatory budgeting in Brazil, we engage in a subnational comparative analysis in which we analyze Brazilian municipalities with more than 50,000 residents. Although a few Brazilian states adopted PB (notably, Rio Grande do Sul, Maranhão, and Piaui), PB has largely been adopted at the municipal level. We choose to focus on municipalities with more than 50,000 for several reasons. First, the vast majority of Brazil's population lives in these municipalities, as between 70 and 80% of the population lived in these cities during the time period analyzed in this book (1990–2020). Second, progressive civil society organizations and political parties that support the expansion of participatory institutions are more likely to be found in larger municipalities (Baiocchi et al., 2011; Torres Ribeiro & Grazia, 2003; Wampler & Avritzer, 2005). Some municipalities with very small populations adopted PB as well (perhaps most famously Icapuí in Northeastern Brazil; see Nylen, 2003), but most of the evidence indicates that, proportionally, PB tends to be adopted more by larger municipalities (Fedozzi et al., 2020, 11; Torres Ribeiro & Grazia, 2003). Third, municipalities with populations over 50,000 are more likely to have sufficient resources and state capacity to implement projects selected by citizens. Relatedly, obtaining reliable information about the use (or not) of participatory budgeting in the more than 5000 Brazilian towns with populations under 50,000 over the 30-year period covered would be virtually impossible; over 4000 of these small municipalities did not have websites as of 2001, nor did they have zoning laws, garbage collection, or a master plan, among other typical urban functions (Da Veiga, 2004).

Subnational comparative analysis provides the opportunity to hold national-level political and economic factors constant (Giraudy et al., 2019; Putnam et al., 1994; Snyder, 2001). Brazil's 1988 Constitution delegated extensive service delivery authority and resources to municipalities, which means that they have a significant role in Brazil's politics. Beginning in the early 1990s, Brazilian municipalities would control roughly 15% of all public revenues, thus giving them a substantial say in service delivery (Montero & Samuels, 2004; Wampler et al., 2020). Although there is great variation across Brazil's five regions, we believe these municipalities are sufficiently similar in terms of authority and resources to make this municipal-focused comparison fruitful.

In this book, we draw on primary research conducted by this book's two authors as well as an excellent and broad body of research conducted by others. Wampler and Goldfrank, separately, started conducting research on Brazil's PB programs in the mid-1990s, when PB programs were first being widely adopted in Brazil. Our research has long sought to understand the variation in why and how governments choose to adopt these programs. Goldfrank and Wampler met in 1999 while both were conducting field research for their doctoral dissertations. Both were training as political scientists (Goldfrank at University of California, Berkeley, and Wampler at University of Texas, Austin) and were interested in similar types of questions: Was the local PB program changing the distribution of power? Were citizens able to claim basic social and political rights through PB?

Wampler's (2007) book, *Participatory Budgeting in Brazil: Cooperation, Contestation and Accountability*, was the first "medium-N" comparison of Brazilian PB cases. The book explains the variation in the performance of eight Brazilian municipalities; some programs were working quite well and other programs struggled to make much of an impact. By focusing on what went well as well as what didn't work, Wampler's study helped to create the foundations for this book. As we demonstrate in this book, changing political incentives altered the rationale for why governments might adopt PB but also why PB programs that have limited impact may discourage governments from adopting it. Goldfrank's (2011) book, *Deepening Local Democracy in Latin America: Participation, Decentralization, and the Left*, compares PB (and related participatory programs) in three cities—Porto Alegre (Brazil), Caracas (Venezuela), and Montevideo (Uruguay)—to assess how different national and local political contexts and program designs produced extensive differences in the programs' effects on citizen engagement and state service provision. By focusing on both incumbent mayors and opposition parties, his work helps provide an understanding of the political contention surrounding participation.

In this book, we also draw on research conducted by others to understand the broader cycles of change. In March 2021, a search on scholar.google.com identified more than 35,000 results when we used the key terms, "Brazil" and "participatory budgeting" (scholar.google.com March 1, 2021). When we moved to google.com, a search using the same key terms found 632,000 results (March 1, 2021). We are obviously unable to cite all of the excellent work done by researchers and civil society activists on PB, but we draw on a broad base of this literature to account for PB's creation, spread, and decline.

PB Censuses

Researchers and civil society activists have consistently sought to document the spread of PB across Brazil, which allows us to draw on a unique dataset linking multiple "PB censuses." The National Forum for Popular Participation conducted the earliest census; it was carried out by university professors and civil society activists, thus allowing for an excellent collaboration that brought together rigorous research design methods with the necessary social networks to identify which municipalities were adopting PB (Torres Ribeiro & Grazia, 2003). The Ford Foundation supported their work on this project (Torres Ribeiro & Grazia, 2003, 13). In 2000, they administered a survey to all municipal governments using PB. To identify municipalities with PB, they drew from their nationwide network of civil society activists a workshop series on popular participation and "snowballing" techniques. They identified 65 municipalities (with more than 100,000 residents) using PB in the 1997–2000 mayoral administrations.[4] This research effort was the first systematic attempt to gather information about the growing number of municipalities using PB. In 2003, Wampler and two research assistants worked with one of the book's authors (Grazia de Grazia) to gather data on the municipalities that used PB during two previous mayoral administrations (1989–1992; 1993–1996).

Wampler and Avritzer (2005) completed a mapping of the 2001–2004 period, which allowed them to capture the changing dynamics of PB. In 2008, Wampler and Avritzer (2009) completed another census focusing on the 2005–2008 period, with the support of the World Bank Institute. In 2012, Paolo Spada completed a survey that covered the 2009–2012 period; Spada also expanded the coverage by gathering information on all municipalities with at least 50,000 residents from 1997 forward. In 2012, Spada, Touchton, and Wampler administered a survey to 94 of the known 100 cases, allowing for a more fine-grained understanding of differences among the PB programs (Touchton et al., 2019; Wampler & Touchton, 2019). In 2016 and 2020, Spada led efforts with the support of the participedia.net to carry out additional censuses, thus giving us a database that covers the 1989–2020 period.

Overall, this means that we have good data on which Brazilian municipalities, with at least 50,000 residents, adopted PB between 1989 and 2020. The inverted U-shaped graph presented at the beginning of this chapter (Fig. 1.1) is based on this database, as is the analysis presented this book. To complement this PB database, we also incorporated publicly available data at the municipal level—such as location, political party of the mayor, and participation in networks—to help us to identify key factors that are associated with why certain municipalities are more likely to adopt PB.

Book Outline

This book contributes to academic and policy debates by drawing from multiple theoretical frameworks to account for PB's broader arc. We first develop, in Chap. 2, an analytical framework that demonstrates how internal, horizontal, and vertical factors best account for why some municipal

[4] Although Torres Ribeiro and Grazia included 65 cases in their book, we use the figure of 67 cases because subsequent research identified 2 cities that were not included in their original database.

governments choose to adopt PB whereas many others chose not to adopt. Chapter 2 thus introduces core theoretical and analytical concepts that we then use to analyze the creation, spread, and decline of PB. The organization of the book largely follows PB's arc in Brazil, beginning with its creation.

Chapter 3 focuses on early cases of PB, which are generally recognized as having formally started in the southern Brazilian city of Porto Alegre in 1989. We note that there were several precursors to Porto Alegre's PB, suggesting that the broad set of ideas behind this innovative institution were present in many locations across Brazil (Pignaton, 2005; Tranjan, 2016). The institutional design and greatest initial successes are situated in Porto Alegre, which helps to explain why Porto Alegre became synonymous with PB.

In Chap. 4, we turn to PB's spread across Brazil. We draw from diffusion theory to account for why PB spread, paying particular attention to the horizontal and vertical networks associated with its spread. Using diffusion theory, we also consider internal factors that made some municipal governments more susceptible to PB adoption. In Chap. 5, we provide an overview of the research that focused on PB-related outcomes. Governments and their allies were supporting the adoption of PB because they believed that the program would improve people's lives. What types of changes were researchers able to identify? Do these findings help to explain both why PB spread across Brazil and why it subsequently declined?

In Chap. 6 we focus on this slow decline. On one hand, fewer and fewer governments were adopting PB after 2004. On the other hand, those governments that were "late adopters" implemented programs that can be categorized as "empty shells" (Wampler, 2009). By this, we mean that these third-generation PB programs were devoid of the resources and design rules that made the initial programs so creative and interesting.

Finally, we conclude the book in Chap. 7 with an effort to draw lessons that can be used in comparative contexts. PB is spreading across the globe, but will other programs share a similar fate? In other words, is Brazil's arc likely to be reproduced elsewhere? If not, why not? Will some PB adopters, especially "late" adopters or those required to use PB, end up creating "empty shells," thus following the Brazilian experience?

References

Abers, R. (1996). From Ideas to Practice: The Partido dos Trabalhadores and Participatory Governance in Brazil. *Latin American Perspectives, 23*(4), 35–53.

Abers, R. (2000). *Inventing Local Democracy: Grassroots Politics in Brazil.* Lynne Rienner.

Alvarez, S. (1990). *Engendering Democracy in Brazil: Women in Transition Politics.* Princeton University Press.

Avritzer, L. (2002). *Democracy and the Public Space in Latin America.* Princeton University Press.

Baierle, S. (1998). The Explosion of Experience: The Emergence of a New Ethical-Political Principal in Popular Movements in Porto Alegre, Brazil. In S. Alvarez, E. Dagnino, & A. Escobar (Eds.), *Cultures of Politics/Politics of Cultures: Re-Visioning Latin American Social Movements* (pp. 118–138). Westview Press.

Baiocchi, G. (2005). *Militants and Citizens: The Politics of Participatory Democracy in Porto Alegre.* Stanford University Press.

Baiocchi, G., & Ganuza, E. (2017). *Popular Democracy: The Paradox of Participation.* Stanford University Press.

Baiocchi, G., Heller, P., & Silva, S. (2011). *Bootstrapping Democracy: Transforming Local Governance and Civil Society in Brazil.* Stanford University Press.

Cabannes, Y., & Lipietz, B. (2017). Revisiting the Democratic Promise of Participatory Budgeting in Light of Competing Political, Good Governance and Technocratic Logics. *Environment and Urbanization, 30*(1), 67–84.

Cameron, M., Hershberg, E., & Sharpe, K. (Eds.). (2012). *New Institutions for Participatory Democracy in Latin America: Voice and Consequence.* Springer.

Da Veiga, J. E. (2004). The Rural Dimension of Brazil. *Estudos Sociedade e Agricultura, 12*(1), 71–94.

Dagnino, E. (1994). *Os Anos 90: Politica e Sociedade no Brasil.* Editora Brasiliense.

Dagnino, E. (1998). The Cultural Politics of Citizenship, Democracy and the State. In S. Alvarez, E. Dagnino, & A. Escobar (Eds.), *Cultures of Politics/ Politics of Cultures: Re-visioning Latin American Social Movements.* Westview Press.

Dias, N. (2018). *Hope for Democracy: 30 Years of Participatory Budgeting Worldwide.* Epopeia Records and Oficina.

Fedozzi, L. (1997). *Orçamento Participativo: Reflexões Sobre a Experiência de Porto Alegre.* Tomo Editorial.

Fedozzi, L., Ramos, M. P., & Gonçalves, F. G. (2020). Orçamentos Participativos: variáveisexplicativas e novos cenários que desafiam a sua implementação. *Revista de Sociologia ePolítica, 73*(28), e005.

Fung, A. (2011). Reinventing Democracy in Latin America. *Perspectives on Politics, 9*(4), 857–871.

Fung, A., & Wright, E. O. (Eds.). (2003). *Deepening Democracy: Institutional Innovations in Empowered Participatory Governance*. Verso.
Genro, T. (1995). *Utopia Possível* (2nd ed.). Artes e Ofícios.
Giraudy, A., Moncada, E., & Snyder, R. (Eds.). (2019). *Inside Countries: Subnational Research in Comparative Politics*. Cambridge University Press.
Goldfrank, B. (2011). *Deepening Local Democracy in Latin America: Participation, Decentralization, and the Left*. Pennsylvania State University Press.
Gonçalves, S. (2014). The Effects of Participatory Budgeting on Municipal Expenditures and Infant Mortality in Brazil. *World Development, 53*, 94–110.
Hunter, W. (2010). *The Transformation of the Workers' Party in Brazil, 1989–2009*. Cambridge University Press.
IBGE. (2001). Pesquisa de InformaçõesBásicasMunicipais 2001. Rio de Janeiro: Instituto Brasileiro de Geografía e Estadística.
IBGE. (2014). Pesquisa de InformaçõesBásicasMunicipais 2014. Rio de Janeiro: Instituto Brasileiro de Geografía e Estadística.
Keck, M. E. (1992). *The Workers' Party and Democratization in Brazil*. Yale University Press.
Marquetti, A. (2003). Democracia, Equidade e Effciencia, o Caso do Orçamento Participativo em Porto Alegre. In L. Avritzer & Z. Navarro (Eds.), *A Inovação Democrática no Brasil: O Orçamento Participativo* (pp. 129–156). Cortez Editores.
McNulty, S. (2011). *Voice and Vote: Decentralization and Participation in Post-Fujimori Peru*. Stanford University Press.
Montambeault, F. (2019). It Was Once a Radical Democratic Proposal: Theories of Gradual Institutional Change in Brazilian Participatory Budgeting. *Latin American Politics and Society, 61*(1), 29–53.
Montero, A. P., & Samuels, D. J. (2004). *Decentralization and Democracy in Latin America*. University of Notre Dame Press.
Nylen, W. (2003). *Participatory Democracy Versus Elitist Democracy: Lessons from Brasil*. Palgrave Macmillan.
Peck, J., & Theodore, N. (2015). *Fast Policy: Experimental Statecraft at the Thresholds of Neoliberalism*. University of Minnesota Press.
Pignaton, F. (2005). *Participação popular na elaboração de orçamentos públicos municipais: a experiência do Espírito Santo, 1983-1994*. EDUFES.
Pogrebinschi, T., & Samuels, D. (2014). The Impact of Participatory Democracy: Evidence from Brazil's National Public Policy Conferences. *Comparative Politics, 46*(3), 313–332.
Porto de Oliveira, O. (2017). *International Policy Diffusion and Participatory Budgeting: Ambassadors of Participation, International Institutions and Transnational Networks*. Palgrave Macmillan.
Putnam, R. D., Leonardi, R., & Nanetti, R. Y. (1994). *Making Democracy Work: Civic Traditions in Modern Italy*. Princeton University Press.

Sandbrook, R. (2014). *Reinventing the Left in the Global South: The Politics of the Possible*. Cambridge University Press.
Santos, B. (1998). Participatory Budgeting in Porto Alegre: Toward a Redistributive Democracy. *Politics and Society, 26*, 461–510.
Santos, B. (Ed.). (2005). *Democratizing Democracy: Beyond the Liberal Democratic Canon*. Verso.
Santos Barreto, D. (2011). Pesquisa de Informacoes Basicas. In R. Pires (Ed.), *Efetividade das Instituições Participativas no Brasil: Estratégias de Avaliação*. IPEA.
Snyder, R. (2001). Scaling Down: The Subnational Comparative Method. *Studies in Comparative International Development, 26*(1), 93–110.
Spada, P. (2020). *Dataset on Brazilian Participatory Budgeting*. Retrieved from https://dataverse.harvard.edu/dataset.xhtml?persistentId=doi:10.7910/DVN/EDSNJS
Torres Ribeiro, A., & Grazia, G. (2003). *Experiência de Orçamento Participativo no Brasil: Periodo de 1997 a 2000*. Editora Vozes.
Touchton, M., & Wampler, B. (2014). Improving Social Well-Being Through New Democratic Institutions. *Comparative Political Studies, 47*(10), 1442–1469.
Touchton, M., Wampler, B., & Peixoto, T. (2019). *Of Governance and Revenue: Participatory Institutions and Tax Compliance in Brazil*. World Bank.
Tranjan, R. (2016). *Participatory Democracy in Brazil: Socioeconomic and Political Origins*. University of Notre Dame Press.
Wampler, B. (2000). *Guide to Participatory Budgeting. International Budget Partnership*. Retrieved from http://www.internationalbudget.org/wp-content/uploads/A-Guide-to-Participatory-Budgets.pdf
Wampler, B. (2007). *Participatory Budgeting in Brazil: Contestation, Cooperation, and Accountability*. Pennsylvania State University Press.
Wampler, B. (2009). Following in the Footsteps of Policy Entrepreneurs: Policy Advocates and Pro Forma Adopters. *Journal of Development Studies, 45*(4), 572–592.
Wampler, B. (2015). *Activating Democracy in Brazil: Popular Participation, Social Justice, and Interlocking Institutions*. University of Notre Dame Press.
Wampler, B., & Avritzer, L. (2004). Participatory Publics: Civil Society and New Institutions in Democratic Brazil. *Comparative Politics, 36*, 291–312.
Wampler, B., & Avritzer, L. (2005). The Spread of Participatory Democracy in Brazil: From Radical Democracy to Good Government. *Journal of Latin American Urban Studies, 7*, 37–52.
Wampler, B., & Avritzer, A. (2009). *The Expansion of Participatory Budgeting in Brazil*. World Bank Report.

Wampler, B., & Touchton, M. (2019). Designing institutions to improve well-being: Participation, deliberation and institutionalisation. *European journal of political research, 58*(3), 915–937.

Wampler, B., McNulty, S., & Touchton, M. (2021). *Participatory Budgeting in Global Perspective.* Oxford University Press.

Wampler, B., Sugiyama, N. B., & Touchton, M. (2020). *Democracy at Work: Pathways to Well-Being in Brazil.* Cambridge University Press.

World Bank. (2008). *Brazil: Toward a More Inclusive and Effective Participatory Budget in Porto Alegre (Report No. 40144-BR).* World Bank.

CHAPTER 2

Analytical Framework: Internal, Horizontal, Vertical

Abstract In this chapter, we draw from the work of Giraudy, Moncada, and Snyder (2019) to develop a multi-level research strategy to assess how internal, horizontal, and vertical factors affect municipal governments' likelihood of adopting participatory budgeting. A multi-level approach permits us to establish an appropriate balance between internal municipal-level government choice, horizontal diffusion, and vertical influences and directives as sources of mayoral decision-making. This multi-level approach permits us to assess how each factor independently and interactively affects governments' decisions to adopt PB, providing an opportunity to develop a comprehensive explanation of PB's arc in Brazil.

Keywords Diffusion • Institutions • Municipal government • Subnational government • Political competition • Democratic innovation • Mayors • Civil society • Networks • Decentralization

Elected governments must decide individually whether or not to adopt PB in Brazil because this political institution was rarely formally codified in law. When governments came into office in a municipality without PB and decided to adopt it, they had to build a participatory system and modify internal administrative processes to support it. When a newly elected government comes into office with a PB program already in place,

B. Wampler, B. Goldfrank, *The Rise, Spread, and Decline of Brazil's Participatory Budgeting*,
https://doi.org/10.1007/978-3-030-90058-8_2

government officials had to decide whether they would maintain or discontinue the existing program. In this book we are interested in identifying factors that are most strongly associated with the decision to adopt PB and, in subsequent mayoral administrations, the decision to re-adopt or discontinue PB. Our theoretical and analytical perspective, then, focuses on the factors that condition government decision-making. In this chapter, we draw from the work of Giraudy et al. (2019) to develop a multilevel research strategy to assess how internal, horizontal, and vertical factors affect municipal governments' likelihood of adopting PB. A multilevel approach permits us to establish an appropriate balance between internal municipal-level government choice, horizontal diffusion, and vertical influences and directives as sources of mayoral decision-making. This multi-level approach permits us to assess how each factor independently and interactively affects governments' decisions to adopt PB, providing an opportunity to develop a comprehensive explanation of PB's arc in Brazil.

Like other participatory institutions, PB is most likely to be adopted at subnational levels because the organizational and informational barriers are lower in comparison to national-level programs. Subnational governments and community organizations generally focus on similar local problems, which encourage them to partner to find local solutions. Therefore, we start with a consideration of internal factors, such as the strength of the Workers' Party and the local configuration of civil society, to help account for government officials' decisions to adopt PB. Municipal governments must actively decide to adopt PB, which means that it is vital to consider how the local political context conditions government officials' decision-making. Of course, we recognize that local political processes are affected by the larger macro-political context. That is, local government decision-making is always nested in a broader context that evolves over time, shaping the incentive structure for local actors. This broader context includes both horizontal and vertical dimensions. Horizontally, municipal government officials are often influenced by other municipalities, as they look for viable solutions to difficult policy and political problems. Sharing information across municipal lines tends to be driven by geography and by ideology. We also examine vertical influences because municipalities are at the lowest level of Brazil's federal system and respond to incentives from state governments and the federal government. Mayors, moreover, are located within political parties that are also national in scope, and some, but not all, Brazilian parties exert influence over the types of policies adopted by local governments.

Internal

The "internal" leg of our analysis situates municipalities as "freestanding units," with political and social dynamics that are unique to each case (Giraudy et al., 2019, 23–25). Our focus on distinctive local dynamics helps illuminate some of the key motivations behind mayors' decisions to adopt specific policies or institutions. Within subnational units, individual executive officeholders—principally mayors in our case—face choices about creating new policies and programs, re-adopting existing policies and programs, or eliminating them. We identify four important local sources of opportunities and constraints that affect the likelihood of PB's adoption: the mayor's political party and broader coalition, the type of party competition, the local configuration of civil society, and the scope of the mayor's resources and authority. The decision to adopt innovative democratic practices is a highly politicized decision, which is why political party-related factors are at the center of our analysis.

Political parties often play key roles in shaping their officeholders' campaign platforms and plans for governing, as well as in creating expectations among the party's base, allies, and voters in general (Baker et al., 2016; Couto, 1995; Hunter, 2010; Mainwaring & Scully, 1995; Power & Zucco, 2009; Samuels, 1999). In multiparty systems, mayoral candidates often need to form an electoral coalition and subsequently a governing coalition in order to succeed. Mayors must thus pay at least some heed to the policy and program demands not only of their party, their base, their social movement allies, and the voting public, but often to those of their coalition partners as well. Even where parties are poorly institutionalized, to varying degrees they still channel and focus societal interests in order to shape the policy agenda (Mainwaring & Scully, 1995, 3). Crucially, parties not only echo the prevailing social structure and political culture, but influence society and politics independently as well through their platforms and policies. Although some innovations occur frequently as politicians respond to societal change and emergence of new interests and problems (Zaremberg et al., 2017), important policy or institutional innovations are more likely when political parties develop strong ideological commitments (Dagnino et al., 2006; Van Cott, 2008) and when organized social groups mobilize around them (Garay, 2020). Over time, of course, as political parties evolve—especially but not only in newer democracies (Baker et al., 2016)—their ideological commitments may change, along with their base, and pressure on mayors to innovate may wane or switch to new domains.

The degree of political competition and the axes around which it revolves also affect how mayors perceive the need to innovate, re-adopt, or discontinue policies. Many scholars argue that competitive electoral districts produce greater policy innovation (Cleary, 2010; Garay, 2020; Rodríguez & Ward, 1994) and that, especially in newer democracies, incoming executives frequently reject the policy innovations of their predecessors (Nickson, 2020). The logic of competition driving innovation is straightforward. With effective competition between parties, voters and social movements have a greater likelihood of affecting the outcome and thus more incentive to press for their demands, and parties have greater interest in being open to their constituencies' preferences by offering innovative responses, for example, to demands for social policy (Garay, 2020) or new forms of participation (Goldfrank & Schneider, 2006). Nonetheless, mayors are also keen to develop their own, or their city's or party's brand, and continuing successful innovations launched by others would dilute the brand (Lupu, 2014; Pasotti, 2010). The branding process is double-edged. When a set of ideas and the parties/group affiliated with it are in ascendance, other parties may be more willing to adopt the ideas. Conversely, when there is a greater political conflict and polarization, rival political parties may choose not to adopt a "best practice" because they don't want to be affiliated with the ideas and policy agenda of a political rival.

Mayors facing policy choices must consider the scope of their authority and the availability of resources they command as well. Those mayors with a greater range of responsibilities, higher revenues, and more freedom to allocate spending will clearly have heightened capacity to innovate compared to those confronting restrictions on their authority and resource generation and allocation. Decentralization is frequently touted for expanding mayors' authority and funding, allowing for innovation to occur (Campbell, 2003), but degrees and types of decentralization vary over time and across countries (Nickson, 2020). Even within countries, decentralization's effects can be uneven across larger and smaller, richer and poorer cities.

The local configuration of civil society is also of crucial importance to the creation of PB because it undergirds the type of social, political, and democracy-enhancing policies that elected governments may adopt while in office. When civil society organizations are more numerous (Putnam's social capital), more active (Escobar & Alvarez, 1992), more democratic (Avritzer, 2002; Dagnino, 1994, 1998), there is a greater likelihood that citizens and CSOs will demand inclusive democratic institutions. Governments interested in developing deep democracy-enhancing projects must obviously first be elected to office, but they then must find partners in civil society that are willing to co-create, or at least participate in, new institutional processes.

Finally, when weighing the costs and benefits of re-adopting or eliminating policies and programs, mayors evaluate how well they are performing and, possibly more importantly, they assess public and elite perceptions of their performance. Innovations initially perceived to be new and exciting may lose their luster as they become routinized (Hacker et al., 2015; Lüchman et al., 2018; Mahoney & Thelen, 2010). Even successful, stable institutions change gradually over time, through layering (adding new elements), displacement by a new model, conversion toward new goals, or policy drift through inattention (Montambeault, 2019, 34; see also Mahoney & Thelen, 2010). If mayors consider prior innovations to have lost their vitality or popularity because of routinization or gradual change, they may implement further changes or abandon them altogether.

Horizontal Diffusion

The "horizontal" leg of our analysis acknowledges that individual municipalities and their governing coalitions are part of a broader grouping of subnational governments. Some elected governments seek to share their innovations, while others seek to learn about what works well in other municipalities, leading in many cases to a horizontal diffusion process across mayoral administrations (Sugiyama, 2012). Diffusion is the uncoordinated spread of a policy or program to interconnected units (Elkins & Simmons, 2005; Mintrom, 1997). Subnational government officials (in states, counties, municipalities, and villages) disseminate information about their own innovative programs horizontally to other units at the same level. Policy entrepreneurs operating in such subnational units often lead the way, working in a "punctured equilibrium" to first craft new policies and then sharing their innovations horizontally with others working at the same level of government (Baumgartner & Jones, 1993; Rogers, 1995). Policy innovations diffuse across the landscape as other governments seek out information on "successful programs" and then adopt those programs that appear capable of solving difficult problems (Porto de Oliveira, 2017).

Previous research identifies four critical factors that make governments open to adopting innovative programs initiated elsewhere. First, when government officials detect that they are part of a changing political context (e.g., democratization, decentralization), political reformers will be more open to adopting new programs in order to address pressing problems. Government officials, working in a fluid policy context, thus look beyond their borders in search of innovative programs (Mintrom, 1997; Peck & Theodore, 2015; Walker, 1969). Second, spatial proximity matters; governments are more likely to adopt programs initiated by "close at hand" governments that are seemingly addressing similar problems (Berry & Berry, 2018; Peck & Theodore, 2015; Porto de Oliveira, 2017). Third, government officials and civil society actors use policy networks to gain information about innovations occurring outside their local area (Porto de Oliveira, 2017; Sugiyama, 2012; Weyland, 2004). Policy networks include individuals and organizations promoting a specific type of policy innovation that addresses seemingly "wicked" problems. Fourth, government officials seek out programs that are more likely to produce policy gains that promote their re-election chances; they would be more likely to adopt programs that are providing clear sources of electoral benefit (Sugiyama, 2012). Thus, we would expect the diffusion of an innovative program to first arise in the geographic region closest to where a pioneering program began, then spread beyond that region through a combination of policy and political networks.

The policy diffusion literature identifies the presence of an "S-shaped" curve whereby diffusion continues until most similar government units adopt comparable programs (Rogers, 1995). Under this scenario, initially, a small number of governments adopt an innovative program, but soon the adoption rate increases and eventually expands to include most available government units; there is a saturation point at which most likely adopters have in fact implemented the program. However, existing research provides much less clarity regarding why some diffusion processes do not fully spread to all available units and which mechanisms limit adoption. Elkins and Simmons argue that "actors may be tempted to opt out of a practice once a certain number of others have adopted it. This will occur if there is some fear of crowding or a desire for uniqueness" (2005, 40–41). Bryan Jones and his co-authors (2014) introduce the idea of a "policy bubble," whereby adoption occurs at a frenzied place in which adoption is part of a fad; the obvious analogies are to housing or stock market bubbles in which buyers continue to buy without clear, rational, evidence-based reasons for doing so. Markets may suddenly burst or may be more like a balloon slowly deflating. We theorize that policy adoption will slow and then, potentially, decline, thus producing an inverted "U-shaped" curve. In this case, diffusion sputters out as governments are no longer willing to adopt. As Fig. 1.1 in this book's introduction demonstrates, the spread of PB is more similar to a bell curve—or an inverted U (∩)—than to the classic S-shaped curve.

Deflation of the adoption rate may stem, theoretically, from a few different sources. First, potential adoptees find it harder and harder to clearly identify the perceived successes of the program. What was initially perceived as producing high governance and electoral pay-offs is found to have much lower pay-offs when more carefully analyzed. Even if the program is found to produce positive policy or community-related outcomes, it may not generate the electoral or governing benefits that convince governments to maintain it (Johannessen, n.d.). As discussed in Chap. 5, most of the research confirming PB's positive impacts was published after PB's adoption began to decline, suggesting that elected governments were more likely to adopt based on an ideological or political commitment rather than using evidence-based decision-making. Additionally, many of the documented changes are relatively small and incremental in nature, such as improving infant mortality or increasing the number of CSOs; although these are important changes to specific communities, the results don't always strongly resonate with the broader electorate.

A second reason that explains the decline in adoption is that the perceived costs of implementing the program are substantially higher than was previously imagined, thus leading government officials to either discontinue it or not adopt it. Third, a program becomes increasingly politicized, which means that some governments will not consider adoption because of the potential negative ramifications (Beer, 2019). As noted above, new democratic institutions are political bodies so it is likely that there will be shifts over time and space in reference to the program's political significance. Fourth, PB adoption rates may also decline due to a generational shift in which reformist politicians and their most active civil society allies are no longer promoting the expansion of civil society. When PB was being founded in the mid-to-late 1980s, the idea of participatory democracy represented a dramatic shift in how policymaking took place. By 2008, there were over 50,000 municipal public policy management councils and dozens of policy conferences, which meant that Brazilian governments and activists could access a much greater number of participatory opportunities; PB wasn't as vital a democratic institution in the mid-2000s as it had been in the late 1980s and 1990s (Pogrebinschi & Samuels, 2014; Santos Barreto, 2011).

In sum, this analysis suggests that a policy can quickly spread based on the broader perception that it can solve multiple social, political, and policy problems. But when a program becomes increasingly politicized (especially in a polarized environment) or when there is a greater disconnect between policy inputs and expected outputs, governments are more likely to choose not to adopt. The S-shaped curve thus peaks and turns into an inverted U.

Vertical

The vertical component of our analytical framework posits that municipal governments are embedded in vertical political and policy networks as well as constrained by federal rules. In some cases, municipal governments may be being directed (formally or informally) by national-level party officials or federal officials to implement a specific type of policy; these mandates may actually decrease local government's authority and flexibility. In addition, municipal governments also contribute innovations upward through these networks. Information may be spread from one municipality to the national government (or political party), which then disseminates this information through its downward-facing networks. Thus, we can also conceptualize the presence of reciprocal exchanges in which the national level influences the local level and vice versa (Giraudy et al., 2019, 26–27).

Elected local officials are often situated in vertical party networks, institutional structures (federalism), and international policy networks that influence their decision-making. These networks and institutional rules both constrain and increase elected officials' options. Vertical party networks involve national-level party officials providing information and party platforms to lower-level officials about the types of programs that elected officials should adopt. When a political party has a strong ideological commitment, when it is programmatic, and when there is significant degree of centralized control, there is an increased likelihood that local governments will follow the directive of the national party. When parties are non-ideological, catch-all, and loosely organized, we could expect that their parties' subnational governments would have much greater freedom to select which, if any, programs they might want to adopt. When local governments are from these catch-all centrist parties, it is more likely that they would be more heavily influenced by horizontal diffusion processes and by political considerations internal to their communities than they would be influenced by the national party.

Subnational governments are embedded in institutional structures that establish their responsibilities, authority, and resources. The degree and type of decentralization matters significantly regarding the type of policies that local governments are more likely to adopt (Falleti, 2005). When subnational or local governments have greater autonomy from direct national control and when they have greater slack resources, they would be more likely to create and/or adopt new programs. When local government's authority shrinks and when they have fewer resources, they are less likely to adopt innovative programs because the costs of experimentation are higher.

Finally, subnational governments are situated within national and international policy networks (Beer, 2019). These networks link global cities (Madrid, São Paulo, Chicago), international organizations (e.g., World Bank, Open Government Partnership, United Nations Development Program, etc.), political parties (e.g., Brazil's Workers' Party in Brazil; Spain's Socialist Party), and more formal social movements and NGOs (IBASE, Instituto Pólis, FASE). Newly created programs that are perceived to be "successful" enter into international and national policy networks as examples of what can be done to address difficult social and political problems. International organizations such as the United Nations and the World Bank often reward innovative programs as "best practices" in order to draw attention to them. Importantly, when leading international organizations highlight a program, this can help legitimize a program that is controversial in its country of origin.

In sum, subnational governments are embedded in vertical networks and institutional structures that directly shape their adoption of innovative programs and institutions. Vertically induced adoption (and the decision *not* to adopt) is driven by different mechanisms, including diffusion (uncoordinated, often led by international policy networks), decentralization (national/federal government changing the rules), and party directives (strong party requiring adoption).

Table 2.1 summarizes the arc of a democratic institution's creation, diffusion, and decline. The multi-level approach allows flexibility to explain the willingness of municipal governments to adopt PB across three distinct

Table 2.1 Explanatory factors across institutional life cycle

	Creation	*Spread*	*Decline*
Internal	**Mayors:** Political opening for democratic innovation led by mayors **Parties:** New party system, including new political parties **Civil society:** Renewal and expansion **Resources:** Fiscal and service-delivery decentralization	**Mayors:** Election of reformist governments "open" to democratic innovations **Parties:** Competitive institution-building by rival parties **Civil society:** CSOs promote participatory politics **Resources:** Decentralization and increase in locally raised taxes, but fiscal recentralization initiated	**Mayors:** Governance pay-offs lower than expected **Parties:** Political pay-offs lower than expected **Civil society**: Weaker support due to demobilization and changing priorities **Resources:** Fiscal recentralization limits municipal autonomy
Horizontal	**Political moment:** Strong political opportunity to innovate **Location:** Governments gather information on more similar, closer programs **Policy networks:** Party and civil society networks promote innovation	**Political moment:** Parties seek to brand themselves as participatory, inclusive, and democratic **Location:** Geographical proximity to well-known cases; then spreads throughout the country **Policy networks:** Good governance policy network spreads ideas	**Political moment:** Growing polarization & corruption scandals discourage cross-party adoption **Policy networks:** Weaker transmission across parties, civil society, and good governance networks
Vertical	**Intra-party:** National party promotes from higher- to lower-level officials **Federalism:** Fiscal and service-delivery decentralization; institutional flexibility to innovate	**Intra-party:** National party continues to promote **Federalism:** Decentralization in some areas, recentralization in other areas **International policy networks:** International organizations promote PB within and beyond Brazil	**Intra-party:** National party no longer actively promotes **Federalism:** Fiscal recentralization deepens **International policy networks:** International organizations' attention turns to promoting PB beyond Brazil

periods. Dynamics shift across the categories because governments are facing different types of pressures depending on the specific moment.

Local political, social, and economic conditions strongly affect the extent to which governments are likely to adopt PB. The "internal" row in Table 2.1 captures the different factors that strongly affect municipal government likelihood to adopt PB. During the "creation" phase, there are a small number of elected governments that are willing to adopt an innovative, radical democratic institution. The internal factors are most important during this first phase, though the vertical factors clearly condition the political opportunities available to governments and CSOs.

The "horizontal" row in Table 2.1 captures the different factors associated with the diffusion of a democratic institution from its original cases to a broader number of cases. The horizontal ties across municipalities best account for the spread of PB across Brazil. These horizontal connections do play a role in the creation phase, but they are much more important in accelerating the spread of PB. The "vertical" row in Table 2.1 illustrates the vital influence of factors that link municipal governments to broader national and international institutions and networks. Municipal governments are linked through networks, party politics, and, of course, federal power-sharing arrangements. In all three periods, we can assert that vertical factors at least moderately affect municipal government decisions to adopt PB.

Finally, Table 2.2 (below) illustrates how the three factors vary in importance across the three periods. During the creation phase, the internal socio-political conditions are the strongest factor that explains why governments would adopt PB. The second strongest factor is the vertical "within party" connections whereby Workers' Party connections were the most important.

During the spread of PB, horizontal connections and vertical connections emerge as being more important than the internal factors. Many elected municipal governments of varying political stripes became

Table 2.2 Relative importance of each factor to explaining the outcome

	Creation	*Spread*	*Decline*
Internal	High	Moderate	High
Horizontal	Limited to moderate	High	Limited
Vertical	Moderate	High	High

connected through policy and political networks, leading them to adopt PB. The Workers' Party strongly encouraged its municipal governments to adopt PB. The local socio-political factors were less important because there was an increase in the number of reformist and leftist governments winning elections. Thus, we can never fully move away from the importance of elections, but the relative increase of leftist governments creates an opportunity for PB to spread. Finally, PB's decline is best explained by internal and vertical factors. On one hand, perceptions of PB's governance and electoral benefits declined over time; on the other, the Workers' Party stopped encouraging PB and recentralization made PB less appealing. Horizontal transmission belts seemed to weaken as well, at the same as political polarization and anti-PT sentiment grew stronger, which limited cross-party dissemination.

Conclusion

This chapter introduces a multi-level analytical framework to explain the creation, spread, and decline of PB in Brazil. To understand the adoption of PB programs by municipal governments, we need to understand how a combination of factors—internal, horizontal, and vertical—influences mayors' decision-making. This approach permits us to explain how mayors' engagement with CSOs and their electoral interests also influenced the creation, spread, and eventual decline of PB. Our approach, we hope, will help the reader to better understand the arc of this innovative democratic institution in Brazil over a 30-year period. We begin, in Chap. 3, by returning to PB's beginnings to explain why PB successfully emerged in Porto Alegre and show how it was a fundamental shift in how local governments engaged with their citizens.

References

Avritzer, L. (2002). *Democracy and the Public Space in Latin America*. Princeton University Press.

Baker, A., Sokhey, A., Ames, B., & Renno, R. (2016). The Dynamics of Partisan Identification When Party Brands Change: The Case of the Workers' Party in Brazil. *The Journal of Politics, 78*(1), 197–213.

Baumgartner, F., & Jones, B. (1993). *Agendas and Instability in American Politics*. University of Chicago Press.

Beer, C. (2019). Multi-level Causation in Gender Policy: Abortion and Violence Against Women Laws in the Mexican States. In A. Giraudy, E. Moncada, & R. Snyder (Eds.), *Inside Countries: Subnational Research in Comparative Politics* (pp. 156–178). Cambridge University Press.

Berry, F., & Berry, W. (2018). Innovation and Diffusion Models in Policy Research. In P. Sabiatier & C. M. Weible (Eds.), *Theories of the Policy Process* (pp. 263–308). Routledge.

Campbell, T. (2003). *The Quiet Revolution: Decentralization and the Rise of Political Participation in Latin American Cities*. University of Pittsburgh Press.

Cleary, M. R. (2010). *The Sources of Democratic Responsiveness in Mexico*. University of Notre Dame Press.

Couto, C. (1995). *O Desafio de ser Governo: O PT na Prefeitura de São Paulo (1988-1992)*. Paz e Terra.

Dagnino, E. (1994). *Os Anos 90: Politica e Sociedade no Brasil*. Editora Brasiliense.

Dagnino, E. (1998). The Cultural Politics of Citizenship, Democracy and the State. In S. Alvarez, S. E. Dagnino, & A. Escobar (Eds.), *Cultures of Politics/ Politics of Cultures: Re-visioning Latin American Social Movements*. Westview Press.

Dagnino, E., Olvera, A., & Panfichi, A. (Eds.). (2006). *A disputa pela construção democrática na América Latina*. UNICAMP.

Elkins, Z., & Simmons, B. (2005). On Waves, Clusters, and Diffusion: A Conceptual Framework. *The Annals of the American Academy of Political and Social Science, 598*(1), 33–51.

Escobar, A., & Alvarez, S. (Eds.). (1992). *The Making of Social Movements in Latin America*. Westview Press.

Falleti, T. G. (2005). A Sequential Theory of Decentralization: Latin American Cases in Comparative Perspective. *American Political Science Review, 99*(3), 327–346.

Garay, C. (2020). Including Outsiders in Latin America. In D. Kapiszewski, S. Levitsky, & D. Yashar (Eds.), *The Inclusionary Turn in Contemporary Latin America*. Cambridge University Press.

Giraudy, A., Moncada, E., & Snyder, R. (Eds.). (2019). *Inside Countries: Subnational Research in Comparative Politics*. Cambridge University Press.

Goldfrank, B., & Schneider, A. (2006). Competitive Institution Building: The PT and Participatory Budgeting in Rio Grande do Sul. *Latin American Politics & Society, 48*(3), 1–31.

Hacker, J. S., Pierson, P., & Thelen, K. (2015). Drift and Conversion: Hidden Faces of Institutional Change. In J. Mahoney & K. Thelen (Eds.), *Advances in Comparative Historical Analysis* (pp. 180–208). Cambridge University Press.

Hunter, W. (2010). *The Transformation of the Workers' Party in Brazil, 1989–2009*. Cambridge University Press.

Johannessen, P. (n.d.). *Visibility and Local Electoral Accountability*. Unpublished Working Paper.
Jones, B., Thomas, H., III, & Wolfe, M. (2014). Policy Bubbles. *Policy Studies Journal, 42*(1), 146–171.
Lüchman, L., Romão, W., & Borba, J. (2018). 30 Years of Participatory Budgeting in Brazil: The Lessons Learned. In N. Días (Ed.), *Hope for Democracy: 30 Years of Participatory Budgeting Worldwide* (pp. 89–103). Oficina.
Lupu, N. (2014). Brand Dilution and the Breakdown of Political Parties in Latin America. *World Politics, 66*(4), 561–602.
Mahoney, J., & Thelen, K. (2010). A Theory of Gradual Institutional Change. In J. Mahoney & K. Thelen (Eds.), *Explaining Institutional Change: Ambiguity, Agency, and Power* (pp. 1–37). Cambridge University Press.
Mainwaring, S., & Scully, T. (1995). *Building Democratic Institutions: Party Systems in Latin America*. Stanford University Press.
Mintrom, M. (1997). Policy Entrepreneurs and the Diffusion of Innovation. *American Journal of Political Science, 41*(3), 738–770.
Montambeault, F. (2019). It Was Once a Radical Democratic Proposal: Theories of Gradual Institutional Change in Brazilian Participatory Budgeting. *Latin American Politics and Society, 61*(1), 29–53.
Nickson, A. (2020). Local Government in Latin America: The Struggle to Overcome Social Exclusion. In R. Kerley, J. Liddle, & P. Dunning (Eds.), *The Routledge Handbook of International Local Government* (pp. 131–148). Routledge.
Pasotti, E. (2010). *Political Branding in Cities: The Decline of Machine Politics in Bogotá, Naples, and Chicago*. Cambridge University Press.
Peck, J., & Theodore, N. (2015). *Fast Policy: Experimental Statecraft at the Thresholds of Neoliberalism*. University of Minnesota Press.
Pogrebinschi, T., & Samuels, D. (2014). The Impact of Participatory Democracy: Evidence from Brazil's National Public Policy Conferences. *Comparative Politics, 46*(3), 313–332.
Porto de Oliveira, O. (2017). *International Policy Diffusion and Participatory Budgeting: Ambassadors of Participation, International Institutions and Transnational Networks*. Palgrave Macmillan.
Power, T. J., & Zucco, C. (2009). Estimating Ideology of Brazilian Legislative Parties, 1990-2005: A Research Communication. *Latin American Research Review, 44*(1), 218–246.
Rodríguez, V., & Ward, P. (1994). Disentangling the PRI from the Government in Mexico. *Mexican Studies/Estudios Mexicanos, 10*(1), 163–186.
Rogers, E. (1995). *Diffusion of Innovations*. Free Press.
Samuels, D. (1999). Incentives to Cultivate a Party Vote in Candidate-Centric Electoral Systems: Evidence from Brazil. *Comparative Political Studies, 32*(4), 487–518.

Santos Barreto, D. (2011). Pesquisa de Informacoes Basicas. In R. Pires (Ed.), *Efetividade das Instituições Participativas no Brasil: Estratégias de Avaliação*. IPEA.
Sugiyama, N. B. (2012). *Diffusion of Good Government: Social Sector Reforms in Brazil*. University of Notre Dame Press.
Van Cott, D. (2008). *Radical Democracy in the Andes*. Cambridge University Press.
Walker, J. (1969). The Diffusion of Innovations Among the American States. *The American Political Science Review, 63*(3), 880–899.
Weyland, K. (Ed.). (2004). *Learning from Foreign Models in Latin American Policy Reform*. Woodrow Wilson Center Press.
Zaremberg, G., Guarneros-Meza, V., & Lavalle, A. G. (Eds.). (2017). *Intermediation and Representation in Latin America: Actors and Roles Beyond Elections*. Springer.

CHAPTER 3

Creation: Workers' Party Governments and Civil Society Allies

Abstract Participatory budgeting consolidated in the southern Brazilian city of Porto Alegre during the early 1990s. The program was quickly adopted by other Brazilian cities, almost all of whom are elected mayors from the Workers' Party. We argue that the presence of a PT mayor offers the strongest explanation for why municipalities adopted PB during the creation period. Eleven of the twelve initial programs were in PT-controlled municipalities. In addition, PB programs were also adopted when was strong support from an expanding leftist civil society. A combination of grassroots social movements and newly professional NGOs worked with citizens and the Workers' Party to support the adoption of PB.

Keywords Democratic innovation • Porto Alegre, Brazil • Workers' Party • Civil society • Collaborative governance • Participatory budgeting

The creation of participatory budgeting is often linked to a single city, Porto Alegre, because it is where PB's institutional design consolidated and where PB received its greatest fame (Abers, 1996; 2000; Avritzer, 2002; Avritzer & Navarro, 2003; Baiocchi, 2005; Santos, 1998). Nonetheless, similar programs proliferated across Brazil prior to and in

B. Wampler, B. Goldfrank, *The Rise, Spread, and Decline of Brazil's Participatory Budgeting*,
https://doi.org/10.1007/978-3-030-90058-8_3

parallel to PB's 1989 "founding" in Porto Alegre (Pignaton, 2005; Pires, 2000; Tranjan, 2016). Notably, in other cities such as Diadema, Ipatinga, Piracicaba, Santo André, Vila Velha, Vitória, and São Paulo, government officials and their civil society allies were experimenting with new ways of incorporating citizens and CSOs into policymaking venues. In terms of democratic institution-building, the 1980s in Brazil represent a critical juncture in which a wide host of policies, programs, and institutions were invented, refined, consolidated, and diffused (Avritzer, 2002; Dagnino, 1994, 1998; Holston, 2009). To explain this critical juncture and why PB developed at this time, a brief re-cap of Brazil's political history in the 1980s is necessary.

The long, drawn-out transition back to a democratic regime took place in Brazil over the 1980s, culminating with the promulgation of a new constitution in 1988 and the direct election of a president in 1989. What is noteworthy about Brazil's transition is that it was promoted by a combination of top-down and bottom-up efforts. As early as 1974, the military government (1964–1985) began to loosen its harsher authoritarian control (O'Donnell et al., 1986). But the 1970s through the early 1980s were marked by extensive labor, social movement, and community-based mobilization that would reshape the terrain of the new democratic regime (Alvarez, 1990; Escobar & Alvarez, 1992; Holston, 2009; Keck, 1992). The labor movement, led by Luiz Inácio Lula da Silva, paralyzed South America's largest industrial complex, thus disrupting the military's timeline for leaving power. In parallel, social movements and community-based organizations expanded their demands for greater inclusion, access to public goods, and democratic rights (Holston, 2009). As Dagnino demonstrates, the concept of citizenship (*cidadania*) became a rallying cry for civil society and labor union activists because it embodied their demands for the expansion of democratic, social, and political rights (Dagnino, 1994, 1998; see also Somers, 2008, Marshall, 1950). Many of these activists took advantage of the military government's 1979 reform, which dissolved the two legally permitted political parties and allowed new parties to form, to establish a new party led by workers. The Workers' Party's base was initially comprised of union members, social movement activists, and members of the small but influential progressive middle class. Many other political parties formed at this time, but the Workers' Party positioned itself as being different, arguing that it sought to radicalize democracy by expanding citizen participation, implement democratic socialism (which was conceived of in different ways by different sectors of the party, but included utilizing the state to reduce poverty and inequality), and generate transparency in government affairs so as to eradicate corruption.

Crucially, this period also included the rewriting of Brazil's constitution. The Constitutional Assembly (1986–1987) drafted a new constitution that introduced three noteworthy changes that are especially pertinent for this book. First, the constitution municipalized service delivery in key areas, such as health, education, and social services. There was an accompanying decentralization of resources to municipalities and states (Montero & Samuels, 2004). This is important because it meant that municipal governments would have far greater resources and responsibilities than their predecessors. Second, there was an expansion of social rights, with the 1988 Constitution guaranteeing Brazilians the right to health care, education, and housing, among others. This created the legal, political, and constitutional framework in which politicians, political parties, and social movement activists would frame their demands. Third, the Constitution and accompanying legislation permitted municipal government to include citizen participation in policymaking venues. This created a "window of opportunity" for governments to invent and adopt new institutions that could directly involve citizens (Avritzer, 2002).[1]

Beyond the Constitutional Assembly, which included mechanisms for social movements to make proposals for the constituents to debate, there was wide experimentation with new democratic institutions at the municipal level during the 1980s. Multiple municipalities, including Lages, Pelotas, Diadema, and Recife, created new venues to incorporate community activists and citizens into public forums where budgets and policies were discussed even before the constitutional changes (Avritzer, 2002; Couto, 1995; Singer, 1996; Tranjan, 2016; Wampler, 2007; Wampler & Avritzer, 2004). Similarly, in São Paulo, the opposition PMDB worked with social movement allies to create new public policy management councils (Holston, 2009; Jacobi, 1989). Thus, the "creation" of PB was part of a broader political moment in which local governments and social movements were actively creating new institutions to solve the problems of public service provision left behind by the military dictatorship (Abers, 1996, 2000; Avritzer, 2002; Baierle, 1998; Baiocchi, 2005; Genro, 1995).

[1] For a somewhat contrasting perspective on the Constituent Assembly, see Tranjan (2016, 225), who argues that it "epitomizes the trend toward more temperate participatory ideals and practices" and that it rejected more radical amendments that would have deepened citizen participation.

We now turn to how internal, horizontal, and vertical factors led to the adoption of 12 PB programs during the initial "creation" phase (1989–1992).

Internal

What was distinctive about these 12 cities that first adopted participatory budgeting? They shared several key traits, including that they were governed by reform-minded mayors eager to engage with citizens through new forms of participation, they were home to social movements that had advocated for democratization and later for new social and political rights during the Constituent Assembly, and they were relatively large, relatively industrialized cities with the ability to take advantage of the new constitution's decentralization of resources and responsibilities to improve public service provision in response to citizen demands. These traits were important for the development of PB, but hardly unique in Brazil's South and Southeast. The distinguishing feature of nearly all these cities is that they were governed by the Workers' Party.

In 1988, the PT won just 15 mayoral elections in municipalities with more than 50,000 residents (out of a possible 465).[2] Of these 15 municipalities, 11 created participatory programs that would eventually be called PB, including 3 state capitals: Porto Alegre (RS), São Paulo (SP), and Vitória (ES).[3] These victories in major cities were somewhat surprising, given that until this point the PT remained a relatively small opposition party, winning very few elections at any level. The 1988 municipal elections and subsequently Lula's strong showing in the 1989 presidential race, which he nearly won, signaled that the PT would be an important competitor in the contest over which political party could best lead Brazil's new democracy. In the 1980s, the PT was but one of several parties trying to establish its democratic bona fides through promoting citizen participation. Its main rivals (and sometimes allies) depended on the city. In the city and state of São Paulo, the strongest competitor was the PMDB

[2] The PT won a total of 36 mayoral offices in 1988 (out of a universe of 4491 municipalities).

[3] Of the four other municipalities, two had short-lived PB-like processes (Campinas and Timoteo). For one city, Rio Grande, no information could be found about PB in the 1989–1992 period, and the mayor abandoned the PT before the end of his term. In the last city, Diadema, the incoming PT mayor discontinued the PB-like process started by his predecessor (Tranjan, 2016, 172).

(which, according to national PT leader, José Álvaro Moisés, had won dozens of state and local elections in 1982 "based on its discourse of participatory democracy").[4] In other cities of the Southeast, the major rival quickly became the PSDB, newly created in 1988. In Rio de Janeiro and further south, in the large cities of Rio Grande do Sul, the PT faced another labor-based party, the PDT, which was launched by the former state governor, labor minister, and leading opponent of the dictatorship, Leonel Brizola.

What's important to emphasize here is that participatory budgeting—and the PT's role in championing it—were not foregone conclusions in the late 1980s and early 1990s. Participatory budgeting was the outcome of a multi-sided struggle between rival parties as well as with social movement and community activists, each with their own views about what local democratic participation should look like.[5] The PT's municipal victories in 1988 were by bare pluralities of just over 30% of the vote in most cities.[6] And these victories arrived on the basis of protest votes against the PMDB, which held both the presidency and 19 of the 25 state capitals at the time (Shidlo, 1998, 73). While the PMDB remained the largest party in the country, its democratic image had been tarnished by its alliance with a conservative party filled with former members and supporters of the dictatorship (the PFL) and by its ineffective government, plagued by hyperinflation, corruption, and rising poverty.

By contrast, during the 1988 election campaigns across Brazil, the PT attempted to highlight its democratic credentials with its call for transparent administration, popular participation, and inverting priorities to favor the poor rather than the rich. Luiza Erundina, the victorious PT candidate in São Paulo, for example, campaigned on the promise to *colocar nas mãos do povo o governo de nossa cidade* (put our city's government in the hands of the people) (Kowarick & Singer, 1993, 203). The PT's leaders in Porto Alegre claimed they wanted to "radically democratize democracy" (Genro & Souza, 1997, 18). For Porto Alegre's first PT mayor Olívio Dutra, this

[4] See the insightful chapter by Moisés (1985, 16) on the debates regarding how PT administrations should organize popular participation in municipal administrations.

[5] The name participatory budgeting (or *orçamento participativo*) itself was not coined until 1990 in Porto Alegre (Silva, 2001, 114), years after versions of it had been attempted by different political parties in multiple cities.

[6] Subsequent elections (e.g., 1992, 1996) would require a run-off if no candidate received at least 50% of the vote, but in the 1988 election, a simple plurality allowed the Workers' Party to win.

meant municipal-level democratization in four senses: *political-institutional*, by creating new channels for direct citizen participation in policymaking; *substantive*, by constantly increasing "the number of residents benefited by urban infrastructure and by municipal public services;" *economic*, by changing tax policy and aiding those living in squatter settlements and shantytowns; and *cultural*, through promotion of a new political culture that would "elevate individuals from mere inhabitants to citizens, conscious of their rights and duties" (Dutra, 1990, 3–5). For the PT, people living in areas without infrastructure were being deprived of their citizenship; "true citizenship required both dignified living conditions and the ability to participate with an equal voice in public decision-making" (Goldfrank, 2011, 40).

While the new PT mayors agreed on the ideas of popular participation to democratize democracy and invert priorities, exactly how to organize these ideas remained subject to intense debate within the party, with rival and allied parties, and with the social movements that the PT hoped to have as partners. The debate over popular participation played out differently in each city, but typically revolved around who should participate (representatives of specific organizations or any and all individual city residents; civil society only or public officials as well), how participation should be organized (territorially or sectorally; through occasional assemblies or conferences or through regularly meeting policy councils), how much autonomy and power should be granted, and whether or how pre-existing participatory venues should be incorporated.[7] In cities like Ipatinga, Porto Alegre, Santo André, and Santos, the PT administration started by holding open public assemblies in different parts of the city to gather citizen demands and was quickly overwhelmed (Abers, 1996, 42). Intra- and inter-party fights—partly over the role of participation—were legion in cities such as São Paulo, where they ultimately led to the downplaying of PB and a focus on pursuing city council harmony; Campinas, where the mayor abandoned the PT partway through his term; and Diadema, where the new PT mayor abandoned the proto-PB process started by his PT predecessor. Ultimately, while all PT-governed cities experimented with multiple participatory formats, the main forms that endured were policy councils, which favored participation by

[7] For accounts of these debates in different cities, see Abers (1996) and Baiocchi (2003). For detailed accounts of these debates in Porto Alegre, see Silva (2001, 100–121), and for Diadema, see Tranjan (2016, 162–174).

representatives of sectoral organizations and public officials, and PB, which favored open, individual participation with a primarily territorial basis.

Both of these formats built on prior experimentation by multiple parties and social movements in the early 1980s. Focusing on PB, Porto Alegre's story is illustrative of the ways in which political parties and community activists competed and collaborated as they debated and designed new forms of citizen participation. Since its founding in 1983, a city-wide federation of neighborhood associations, UAMPA, had been promoting direct citizen involvement in public policy venues, including both sectoral popular councils for the municipal government's different administrative departments and direct input into the entire municipal budget (Baierle, 1998; Fedozzi, 1997; Genro, 1995; Schmidt, 1994; UAMPA, 1989, 3, 71). At UAMPA's congress in 1985, the mayoral candidates from the PMDB, PDT, and PT all focused on "popular participation" in their speeches (Silva, 2001, 84–85). The PMDB candidate (who was in an alliance with the PFL as well as with the two Communist parties, the PCB and PC do B) promised to bring the "community budget" experience from the city of Pelotas, where a PMDB mayor governed, to Porto Alegre if elected; the PDT candidate promised direct participation with his slogan *o povo no governo* ("the people in the government"); and the PT candidate promised popular councils (Silva, 2001, 84–85, 93). After the PDT candidate won, his administration failed to implement a popular councils proposal supported by UAMPA, and he lost their support (Goldfrank, 2011, 81).

When the Workers' Party came into office in 1989 (with the support of the PCB), therefore, UAMPA was well-positioned to work closely with this new government to better connect it to community groups across the city. The Workers' Party was in a minority position in the municipal legislature; it had unclear levels of public support given that 66% of voters had selected other parties' candidates for mayor. Thus, the PT had strong electoral and governance incentives to work closely with UAMPA to try to expand its connections to different communities across Porto Alegre. Nonetheless, partly because UAMPA's leadership had stronger ties to other political parties, relations between the PT and UAMPA did not go well at first. In fact, after intense debates over how to design citizen participation in the budget process—including how many districts to include, how to prioritize projects and neighborhoods, and who could participate—involving multiple community organizations and district-level popular councils as well as PT factions, UAMPA refused to send representatives to the budget assemblies for two years, partly because it lost the fight to keep PB exclusive to UAMPA members and partly because its PDT-linked leaders attempted a boycott (Goldfrank, 2011, 171–172, 184). This messy, contested process nonetheless eventually resulted in the Porto Alegre model of PB, entailing the regular holding of 2 rounds of open public assemblies in 16 districts, voting on budget priorities, a formula weighting population size and public service needs to help allocate resources across districts, and a set of district budget forums and a municipal budget council that meet continuously.

Although Porto Alegre's PB case is often cited as the "founding program," at least 11 other medium or large cities also adopted some form of PB during the 1989–1992 mayoral period and labeled it as such. Ten of these cities were governed by the Workers' Party. The internal dynamics described above were roughly similar across other cities—a reformist political party aligning itself with social movements as it competes with other parties to demonstrate its democratic qualifications, leading the government to initiate new forms of engaging the population (Abers, 1996, 2000; Avritzer, 2002; Avritzer & Navarro, 2003; Couto, 1995; Jacobi, 1989; Wampler, 2007). The other municipalities adopting PB were all located in the Southeast (Vitória, Vila Velha, Piracicaba, Ipatinga, Jaboticabal, João Monlevade, Angra dos Reis, Santos, Santo André, São Bernardo do Campo, and São Paulo), which was Brazil's industrial base and, not coincidentally, where the Workers' Party was strongest.

The case of Vila Velha is the outlier, but one that confirms the general rule that reformist political parties and their deep connections to a revitalized civil society helped to generate support for public participation. During the 1989–1992 period, Vila Velha is the only municipal government that used PB but was not governed by the Workers' Party; instead, it was governed by the centrist PSDB. Yet closer examination reveals that Vila Velha started its version of "Participatory Budgeting" in 1984 when it held a "Municipal Budgeting Assembly" that brought community leaders and citizens together to discuss budget priorities (Pignaton, 2005; Torres & Bodart, 2017, 43). In 1985, under a PMDB mayor, the municipality passed a law (#2247/1985) requiring citizen participation in the annual budget process. The law was proposed by a member of the Brazilian Communist Party (PCB), suggesting that the effort to incorporate citizens into budget-making was part of a leftist political project. Moreover, after the PMDB mayor resigned in 1987, a PT candidate won a special election and expanded participation in the budgeting process as mayor; the PT mayor of the neighboring city of Vitória then used Vilha Vela's experience as a reference point for PB (Paste, 2018, 87). Broadly, this case demonstrates that, though the PT was clearly crucial to the development of participatory budgeting, in fact PB was the product of multiple "authors," all of whom were engaged in Brazil's gradual democratization process in the 1980s, both competing and collaborating across a spectrum of leftist and centrist civil society organizations and political parties.

Horizontal

Civil society activists and social movements took advantage of the "window of opportunity" created by democratization during the 1980s and early 1990s to promote direct citizen engagement, promotion of citizenship rights, and new participatory institutions (Alvarez et al., 1998; Avritzer, 2002; Avritzer & Navarro, 2003; Holston, 2009). Within civil society, there was an expansion of social movements, including activist neighborhood associations, movements for education, health, and housing, and Christian Base Communities, and a proliferation of NGOs such as *Instituto Pólis, IBASE, Instituto Cajamar,* and *FASE.* The NGOs served as transmission belts for ideas associated with popular participation and citizenship and were embedded in progressive politics, working within civil society, with progressive political parties, and with centrist and leftist municipal administrations (Villas Boas, 1994). These organizations were autonomous from but also linked to the Workers' Party, which itself was deeply embedded in civil society (Escobar & Alvarez, 1992; Keck, 1992). We turn to a brief description of several of these organizations to illuminate their development and reach, showing how collectively they formed a policy network that facilitated the diffusion of PB in cities in the Southeast.

The *Instituto Cajamar*, located within a short drive of São Paulo, was a key center for the development of social movement and PT leaders. Founded in 1987, this institute connected policy and political worlds (FASE, CUT, Instituto Pólis, the PT, and social movements). Founding members included Paulo Freire (world-renowned scholar and education activist), Gilberto Carvalho (close aide to future Presidents Lula and Dilma), Pedro Pontual (under President Lula, he would direct the national participatory programs), Olívio Dutra (Porto Alegre's first PT mayor), and Luiza Erundina (São Paulo's first PT mayor). The *Instituto Cajamar* disseminated information about participation, institutional reform, and urban renewal (Caetano, 1995; Wampler interviews 1995 and 1996). For example, prior to the 1988 municipal elections, the Instituto Cajamar organized a seminar for PT candidates for mayor and city councilor (including future Porto Alegre mayor, Olívio Dutra) titled "Local Power and Popular Participation" that highlighted citizen participation in budgeting in Vila Velha (Silva, 2001, 91–92). After the 1988 elections, *Instituto Cajamar* served as a hub for PT officials from various cities. According to the PB coordinator for Vitória at the time: "We held meetings to see the evolution of the experiences. We went there to exchange experiences and enrich the proposals that the PT administrations were doing at the time" (Cristina Sampaio, interviewed by Paste, 2018, 88).

During the 1980s, *Instituto Pólis*, a progressive think tank, actively promoted the expansion of citizen participation in public policies. *Pólis* was a new type of think tank and NGO in Brazil, serving as a public policy institute that published dozens of studies of local administrations utilizing new participatory mechanisms but also directly working in alliance with social movements and community organizations to advocate for specific social policies and participatory innovations. A key ally of the Instituto Pólis was Celso Daniel, an economics professor at one of Brazil's leading universities (FGV), as well as the PT-affiliated mayor of Santo André, a city that would adopt participatory budgeting during his first term (1989–1992) in office.[8] Pedro Pontual, who ran PB under Mayor Daniel in Santo Andre, worked with Instituto Pólis. Simply put, there was an intermixing of people in municipal administrations, NGOs, think tanks, and universities.

In parallel, an emerging NGO community led by FASE and IBASE also disseminated information about PB processes and offered training to civil society participants (Wampler interviews 1996 and 1998). During the late 1980s, FASE had regional affiliates in Porto Alegre, Vitória, and São Paulo, all of which would adopt PB during the early years. These organizations were more focused on providing direct support to communities (distinct from *Polis*, which initially was more of a think tank than a service-delivery NGO). In Porto Alegre and Vila Velha, for example, FASE (1989; 1990; 1992) conducted interviews with local activists involved in the first years of PB and published reports on their critiques of

[8] Interestingly, Celso Daniel wrote his urban planning master's thesis at FGV on popular participation in budget decisions in the cities of Osasco and Boa Vista during the early 1980s (Silva, 2001, 91, 261).

the process as well as their proposals for how to improve it. FASE, with its affiliates in São Paulo, Vitória, and Recife, shared information about PB in Porto Alegre and Vila Velha, serving as a horizontal transmission belt.

Together, these NGOs formed the National Forum for Popular Participation (FNPP) in 1990. Its members included key NGOs: *IBASE* (based in Rio de Janeiro), *FASE* (six branch offices across Brazil), *Cidade* (Porto Alegre), *INESC* (Brasília), and *Pólis* (São Paulo). Their workshops and meetings were held at the Instituto Cajamar, helping create informal connections among party and policy activists who were seeking to create new democratic institutions. In 1993, the FNPP modified its name to be the National Forum for Popular Participation in Municipal Administrations, signaling the institutionalization of new forms of popular participation. Thus, during PB's early years, information about PB was disseminated through parallel and overlapping networks of progressive and leftist civil society and policy activists located primarily in Brazil's Southeast region. (The impact of the FNPP is covered more extensively in Chap. 4.)

Vertical

The vertical factors present during this first phase are institutional, as Brazil began a major decentralization project, and choice-oriented, as the PT began to develop and promote a distinctively *petista* way of governing that included participatory budgeting as a central means of reversing or "inverting" government priorities away from the upper classes and toward the popular sector.

As noted above, the new constitution, by extending greater resources and additional responsibilities downward, increased the significance of Brazilian municipal governments. The reorganization of Brazil's federal structures provided an expansion of opportunities, giving newly elected governments a historic opening to recreate basic governance structures. Municipal governments came to control upward of 15% of all public spending (Montero & Samuels, 2004), and they were given responsibility for basic service delivery and infrastructure. Though many service provision responsibilities were and are still shared with the national- or state-level governments, municipalities became significant players. Policy and institutional experimentation were rampant across Brazil as local governments and their civil society allies designed new programs and institutions (Holston, 2009, Jacobi, 1989, Sugiyama, 2012). PB was one significant innovation created during this period, but there were others, including

Bolsa Escola (one of the first conditional cash transfer programs in Latin America)and *Programa de Saúde Familiar* (a family health program that helps ensure that universal healthcare reaches all families) (Sugiyama, 2012). Beyond PB, local governments also experimented with refining and engaging policy councils and policy conferences.

Municipal administrations led by the PT were especially active in this kind of experimentation and, during this period, the party created the National Secretariat of Institutional Affairs (SNAI) "as a deliberate effort to learn from PT experiences and build a coherent and pragmatic political program" (Tranjan, 2016, 203); or as Hunter (2010, 94) argues, as a way "to define some uniformity in the policies to be enacted by PT-governed cities and to establish mechanisms for their collaboration and coordination." In parallel to the work done by the Instituto Cajamar, the SNAI held seminars for party leaders, including a special national meeting in 1991 dedicated to evaluating the PT's municipal administrations. One outcome of these meetings was the publication of a book organized by the SNAI's director, *O Modo Petista de Governar* (Bittar, 1992). This book highlights participatory budgeting, specifically as practiced in Porto Alegre, as a model for successfully translating participatory ideals into democratic local government. In sum, during this period, as the Workers' Party was developing itself into a unified organization in which its elected governments would implement similar programs, participatory budgeting came to be viewed by PT leaders as particularly well-suited for addressing two key problems faced by newly elected governments: Developing connections to a broader range of constituents (voters) and using the state apparatus to solve crucial problems of public service provision.

When the PT won elections in medium and large cities during the 1989–1992 mayoral term, the mayors nearly always adopted PB. Each city had its particular version of implementing PB, but it was Porto Alegre's model that drew national and international attention, mostly because it was the largest city in which the government won consecutive elections. In other key cities, such as São Paulo, Santos, and Santo André, PT governments adopted PB in 1989 or 1990, but the party lost the 1992 election and the new governments discontinued PB.

It is also important to emphasize that the creative developmental process leading up to PB took place in specific cities that were especially poised to take advantage of the new constitution. The 1988 Constitution and accompanying legislation decentralized basic service delivery responsibilities to municipal and state governments. Municipal governments in

Brazil were given the responsibility of providing basic infrastructure (e.g., street paving and lighting, sewage), health and education, transportation, and housing, among other services. Brazilian cities during the 1980s were marked by major inequalities; wealthier communities had access to sewage, electricity, water, and paved streets while poorer communities often lacked these same basic services. Brazil's urban areas were marked by extensive informality, in which residents "invaded" or "claimed" private and public lands that were not developed (Holston, 2009). Under previous governance systems, municipal, state, and federal governments built infrastructure in business and industrial districts as well as in upper-income communities, yet often ignored infrastructure needs in poorer, peripheral areas. PB was established just as municipal governments began to benefit from the greater resources and responsibilities afforded by the new constitution, which allowed interested governments to invest in poor communities to better address the lack of basic public goods. Importantly, the decentralization afforded greater opportunities for larger municipalities—those that could raise additional revenues through property and sales taxes as well as being able to draw on existing public infrastructure (e.g., schools, maintenance equipment, etc.). Less densely populated and poor municipalities were at a substantial fiscal and infrastructure disadvantage, thus resulting in lower levels of state capacity. State capacity is crucial to PB programs because governments need to be able to implement projects selected by participants.

Conclusion

In this chapter, we argue that the presence of a PT mayor offers the strongest explanation for why municipalities adopted PB during the creation period. Eleven of the twelve initial programs were in PT-controlled municipalities. The PT was a unique party in Brazil—it was a collective of unions, civil society organizations, and a small, but influential, progressive middle class. Unlike most of its counterparts, the PT developed a clear programmatic agenda. At the municipal level, PT governments sought to "invert" how previous governments allocated resources as well as how decisions were made. The hope, among PB advocates, was that PB would invert spending by increasing public works projects in poor communities, and also invert the political power within the municipalities by increasing the relative strength of individuals and groups from poor communities.

Porto Alegre is often identified as the "founder" of PB, which we believe to partially correct. The core institutional design features of PB clearly consolidated in Porto Alegre and it had some of the earliest successes (high mobilizations in years 3 and 4; projects implemented in poor communities). But Porto Alegre built on previous experiences that were developed across Brazil during the 1980s. The simultaneous development of PB in other cities was largely done under the auspices of the Workers' Party, which was competing with other parties to demonstrate its democratic, participatory credentials. Party leaders were attempting to build a different type of politics, which led them to adopt policies that they believed would transform the process through which public decision-making took place as well as the outputs.

During the 1980s and 1990s, the Workers' Party and their allies in civil society built a policy network that promoted participation, transparency, oversight, and the allocation of additional resources to poor communities. The Workers' Party and these autonomous networks would lead the effort to spread PB across Brazil. In the following chapter, we turn to PB's spread across Brazil between 1993 and 2004.

References

Abers, R. (1996). From Ideas to Practice: The Partido dos Trabalhadores and Participatory Governance in Brazil. *Latin American Perspectives, 23*(4), 35–53.

Abers, R. (2000). *Inventing Local Democracy: Grassroots Politics in Brazil.* Lynne Rienner.

Alvarez, S. (1990). *Engendering Democracy in Brazil: Women in Transition Politics.* Princeton University Press.

Alvarez, S., Dagnino, E., & Escobar, A. (Eds.). (1998). *Cultures of Politics/Politics of Cultures: Re-visioning Latin American Social Movements.* Westview Press.

Avritzer, L. (2002). *Democracy and the Public Space in Latin America.* Princeton University Press.

Avritzer, L., & Navarro, Z. (2003). *A inovação democrática no Brasil: o orçamentoparticipativo.* Cortez Editora.

Baierle, S. (1998). The Explosion of Experience: The Emergence of a New Ethical-Political Principal in Popular Movements in Porto Alegre, Brazil. In S. Alvarez, E. Dagnino, & A. Escobar (Eds.), *Cultures of Politics/Politics of Cultures: Re-Visioning Latin American Social Movements* (pp. 118–138). Westview Press.

Baiocchi, G. (Ed.). (2003). *Radicals in Power: The Workers' Party (PT) and Experiments in Urban Democracy in Brazil.* Zed Books.

Baiocchi, G. (2005). *Militants and Citizens: The Politics of Participatory Democracy in Porto Alegre.* Stanford University Press.

Bittar, J. (1992). *O modo petista de governar*. Camargo Soares.
Caetano, M. E. (1995). *Educação para Transformação ou para Mudar as Algemas de Mão? Um Estudo sobre Educação e Formação no Insituto Cajamar – INCA*. Master's Thesis, UNICAMP.
Couto, C. (1995). *O Desafio de ser Governo: O PT na Prefeitura de São Paulo (1988-1992)*. Paz e Terra.
Dagnino, E. (1994). *Os Anos 90: Politica e Sociedade no Brasil*. Editora Brasiliense.
Dagnino, E. (1998). The Cultural Politics of Citizenship, Democracy and the State. In S. Alvarez, S. E. Dagnino, & A. Escobar (Eds.), *Cultures of Politics/Politics of Cultures: Re-visioning Latin American Social Movements*. Westview Press.
Dutra, O. (1990). *A hora das definições estratégicas: um roteiro para orientar as mudanças políticas, institucionais e administrativas na Prefeitura Municipal de Porto Alegre*. Administração Popular.
Escobar, A., & Alvarez, S. (Eds.). (1992). *The Making of Social Movements in Latin America*. Westview Press.
Fedozzi, L. (1997). *Orçamento Participativo: Reflexões Sobre a Experiência de Porto Alegre*. Tomo Editorial.
Genro, T. (1995). *Utopia Possível* (2nd ed.). Artes e Ofícios.
Genro, T., & Souza, U. (1997). *Orçamento Participativo: a experiência de Porto Alegre*. Fundação Perseu Abramo.
Goldfrank, B. (2011). *Deepening Local Democracy in Latin America: Participation, Decentralization, and the Left*. Pennsylvania State University Press.
Holston, J. (2009). *Insurgent Citizenship: Disjunctions of Democracy and Modernity in Brazil*. Princeton University Press.
Hunter, W. (2010). *The Transformation of the Workers' Party in Brazil, 1989–2009*. Cambridge University Press.
Jacobi, P. (1989). *Movimentos Sociais e Políticas Públicas: Demands por Saneamento Básico e Saúde. São Paulo, 1974-84*. Cortez Editora.
Keck, M. E. (1992). *The Workers' Party and Democratization in Brazil*. Yale University Press.
Kowarick, L., & Singer, A. (1993). A Experiência do Partido dos Trabalhadores na Prefeitura de São Paulo. *Novos Estudos CEBRAP, 35*, 205–220.
Marshall, T. H. (1950). *Citizenship and Social Class*. Cambridge University Press.
Moisés, J. (1985). Poder Local e Participação Popular. In P. Dallari (Ed.), *Política Municipal*. Mercado Aberto and Fundação Wilson Pinheiro.
Montero, A. P., & Samuels, D. J. (2004). *Decentralization and Democracy in Latin America*. University of Notre Dame Press.
O'Donnell, G., Schmitter, P., & Whitehead, L. (Eds.). (1986). *Transitions from Authoritarian Rule: Prospects for Democracy: Conference*. Johns Hopkins University Press.
Paste, J. (2018). *Participação Social na Gestão e na Configuração Territorial de Vitória - 1985 a 2014* (Master's Dissertation). Universidade Federal do Espírito Santo.

Pignaton, F. (2005). *Participação popular na elaboração de orçamentos públicos municipais: a experiência do Espírito Santo, 1983-1994*. EDUFES.
Pires, V. (2000). *Participação de Sociedade nos Processos Orçamentários: a Experiência Brasileira Recente*. Presented at the XXVVI Seminario Internacional de Presupuesto Publico, October 22–26, 2000.
Santos, B. (1998). Participatory Budgeting in Porto Alegre: Toward a Redistributive Democracy. *Politics and Society, 26*, 461–510.
Schmidt, D. (1994). *A 'desidiotização' da cidadania: a formação do cidadão para a coisa pública, através da sua participação no processo do Orçamento Participativo de Porto Alegre, entre 1989 e 1992* (Master's Dissertation). Universidade Federal do Rio Grande do Sul.
Shidlo, G. (1998). Local Urban Elections in Democratic Brazil. In H. Dietz and G. Shidlo (Eds.), *Urban Elections in Democratic Latin America*. Scholarly Resources.
Silva, M. (2001). *Construção da "Participação Popular": Análise comparativa de processos e participacão social na discussão pública do orçamento em municipios da Região Metropolitana de Porto Alegre/RS* (Ph.D. Dissertation). Universidade Federal do Rio Grande do Sul.
Singer, P. (1996). *Un Governo de Esquerda para Todos: Luiza Erundina na Prefeitura de São Paulo (1989-1992)*. Editora Brasiliense.
Somers, M. (2008). *Genealogies of Citizenship: Markets, Statelessness and the Right to Have Rights*. Cambridge University Press.
Sugiyama, N. B. (2012). *Diffusion of Good Government: Social Sector Reforms in Brazil*. University of Notre Dame Press.
Torres, K., & Bodart, C. (2017). Ação Comunicativa eo Orçamento Participativo: A Experiência De Vila Velha/ES. *Alabastro, 4*, 32–55.
Tranjan, R. (2016). *Participatory Democracy in Brazil: Socioeconomic and Political Origins*. University of Notre Dame Press.
UAMPA. (1989). *Participação na elaboração do orçamento municipal*. Mimeograph.
Villas Boas, R. (1994). *Participação Popular nos Governos Locais*. Instituto Pólis.
Wampler, B. (2007). *Participatory Budgeting in Brazil: Contestation, Cooperation, and Accountability*. Pennsylvania State University Press.
Wampler, B., & Avritzer, L. (2004). Participatory Publics: Civil Society and New Institutions in Democratic Brazil. *Comparative Politics, 36*, 291–312.

CHAPTER 4

The Spread of PB: The Workers' Party and Beyond

Abstract Participatory budgeting spread across Brazil during the 1990s and 2000s, reaching its height in 2004. Our focus in this chapter is on this spread. What were the drivers behind the adoption of PB? What were the political incentives for governments to adopt PB? In this chapter, we argue that vertical connections between the national PT and its municipal governments as well as horizontal connections across municipalities help account for PB's spread during the 1993–2004 period. Importantly, the Workers' Party and its leftist allies were at the heart of PB's spread across Brazil. In addition, a "Good Governance" network that promoted policy innovations was associated with the adoption of PB by centrist and center-right political parties.

Keywords Diffusion • Workers' Party • Decentralization • Good governance • Participatory budgeting • Networks

Participatory budgeting spread across Brazil during the 1990s and 2000s, reaching its height in the 2001–2004 term, when 138 municipalities adopted it.[1] Across four mayoral periods (1989–1992, 1993–1996,

[1] We note that the intensive international spread of PB began in the post-2004 period, which means that PB was already in decline in Brazil as it began its rapid spread around the globe.

B. Wampler, B. Goldfrank, *The Rise, Spread, and Decline of Brazil's Participatory Budgeting*,
https://doi.org/10.1007/978-3-030-90058-8_4

Table 4.1 Total # of PB programs in municipalities with more than 50,000 residents

	Total PB programs	*# led by PT*	*# led by other leftist parties*	*# led by PMDB*	*# led by PSDB*	*# led by conservative parties*
1989–1992	12	11	0	0	1	0
1993–1996	31	15	5	4	7	0
1997–2000	67	26	14	3	15	9
2001–2004	138	55	30	12	17	24
2005–2008	126	47	34	10	15	20
2009–2012	99	50	17	14	8	10
2013–2016	79	33	22	9	10	5
2017–2020	43	3	13	5	7	15
Total	595	240	135	57	80	83

Leftist parties include PSB, PV, PC do B, PDT, PPS; Conservative parties include PFL (DEM), PPB (PP), PTB, PL, and several smaller parties

1997–2000, 2001–2004), there was an increase in each mayoral term in the total number of programs as well as the total number of new municipalities adopting it. Across the period covered in this book (1989–2020), 48% (278 of 578) of Brazilian municipalities with more than 50,000 residents adopted PB. As Table 4.1 below demonstrates, the most significant increase in adoption took place between 1993 and 2004. Of the 278 municipalities that used PB, 177 adopted PB by 2004, which is 64% of all adoptions. Our focus in this chapter is on this spread. What were the drivers behind the adoption of PB? What were the political incentives for governments to adopt PB? Did specific political parties or civil society organizations promote PB? What local political conditions facilitated this process?

The spread of PB across Brazil took place in a broader national context framed by the stabilization of the economy in 1994 with the *Real* plan, the election of centrist Fernando Henrique Cardoso to the presidency, and the contrasting processes of decentralization and then recentralization of resources and service delivery to states and municipalities (Eaton & Dickovick, 2004). This was a period of democratic institution-building and consolidation (Avritzer, 2002; Keck, 1992; Mainwaring & Scully, 1995). During this period, reformist subnational governments continued experimenting with democratic institutions and, in several regions, placed a strong emphasis on promoting "Good Governance" (Tendler, 1997).

Returning to the three analytical categories (internal, vertical, horizontal), the election of a Workers' Party government is the most important factor that explains why a municipal government would adopt PB between 1993 and 2004 (Bezerra, 2016; Spada, 2014; Wampler, 2008). We find that vertical connections between the national PT and its municipal governments as well as horizontal connections across municipalities help account for PB's spread during the 1993–2004 period (Wampler, 2009). It is thus a combination of internal (winning elections), vertical (national party including PB as part of its platform), and horizontal relationships ("popular participation" and "good governance" networks) that explains why governments adopt PB.

Table 4.1 demonstrates that the Workers' Party and other leftist parties account for the majority of PB adoptions. Of the 595 mayoral governments using PB, 63% were led by the Workers' Party or other leftist parties. This is clear and compelling evidence that Brazil's leftist political parties adopted PB when they were in government. In addition, 60% of first-time adoptions were led by governments under the Workers' Party or other leftist parties. Based on these data, the reader might assume that the Workers' Party was a major political party in municipal governments. The opposite, in fact, is true. The Workers' Party controlled just than 5% of the larger municipal governments between 1997 and 2000 and 11% between 2001 and 2004. Thus, the PT didn't often win municipal elections, but when they did, they were highly likely to adopt PB.

As we explain in greater detail below, the Workers' Party and its leftist allies were at the heart of PB's spread across Brazil. There are different mechanisms at work, including the ability of the Workers' Party to win mayoral elections, as well as complementary horizontal and vertical connections among Workers' Party governments and party leaders. But the spread of PB isn't simply about the political left's willingness to adopt. We also see some mayors from the two largest centrist parties (PMDB and PSDB) adopting PB, and by the end of this period, a number of mayors from conservative parties began adopting PB as well. It is during PB's spread that we begin to see a new phenomenon—governments adopting PB for short-term political and policy advantages but only occasionally fully investing the necessary time, support, and resources to produce high-functioning institutions. In some municipalities, local governments work hard to generate the build vibrant programs, but in other cases, local governments invest minimal time and effort to support PB programs (Baiocchi et al., 2011; Baiocchi & Ganuza, 2017; Lüchman et al., 2018; Wampler,

2007, Chapter 5; Wampler et al., 2021). We turn now to the three pillars of our analytical framework; we show how internal, horizontal, and vertical factors influence municipal governments' decisions to adopt PB.

Internal

As developed in Chap. 2 (see Table 2.1), there are four analytical categories that we utilize to best explain governments' incentives to adopt PB: the mayor, parties, civil society, and resources. We begin by looking mayor and the PT. When the PT won municipal elections during the 1990s and early 2000s, its mayors adopted PB. The primary factor that explains the adoption of PB was the Workers' Party being elected to the Mayor's office. In addition, when the PT was in the electoral coalition that elected the mayor, the municipalities also tended to adopt PB at a higher rate. Across the 1993–2004 period, PT governments adopted the largest number of new PB programs and 90% of PT governments in larger cities adopted PB between 1993 and 2004.[2] Across the 1990s, the PT mostly won mayoral races in municipalities located in the south and southeastern regions of Brazil. These municipalities are wealthier than the mean for their respective states, have larger middle classes, have larger per capita budgets, and have greater numbers of private and public-sector unions (Hunter, 2010; Wampler, 2008).

In parallel, when other leftist parties won mayoral elections during the 1993–2004 period, they also adopted PB, albeit at lower rates than the PT. Sixteen percent of municipalities under (non-PT) leftist parties adopted PB during the 1997–2000 period, and 35% did so during the 2001–2004 period, which suggests that other leftist political parties were open to adopting PB but weren't as committed to PB as was the Workers' Party. Although other leftist parties were sometimes political rivals with the PT, they often adopted similar policies because they shared, with the PT, a broad commitment to participation, the expansion of democratic citizenship rights (***cidadania***), citizen empowerment, and deepening democracy. Unsurprisingly, these parties were those most likely to form electoral coalitions with the PT. Although we lack electoral coalition data for most of the 1993–2004 period, we do have it for the last term, and it

[2] Brazil's federal electoral body (TSE) provides results on all elections beginning in 1994. For the 1988 and 1992 elections, our data is incomplete. We know where the PT won mayoral elections but we don't have reliable information on other political parties' victories.

shows that, during this 2001–2004 period, of the 30 leftist governments that implemented PB without a PT mayor, the PT was involved in 21 as a coalition partner (70%). For example, in the city of Rio Claro, in the interior of the state of São Paulo, a Green Party government was elected with a focus on improving the municipality's environment. The Vice-Mayor was from the Workers' Party. The municipal government adopted PB at the behest of the Vice-Mayor because this was an important issue for the local PT (Wampler, 2007, Chap. 5).

However, most municipal elections in Brazil are won by centrist and conservative political parties; the vast majority of these governments didn't adopt PB. Following the PT, the two political parties that adopted the most PB programs were the centrist, catch-all parties, the PMDB, and PSDB. The percentage of PMDB governments adopting PB between 1997 and 2004 was just 8% and the PSDB was about 15%. The comparatively high rate of cities with Workers' Party mayors adopting PB (90% of PT governments) suggests that the PT mayors were not only responding to citizen demands for greater participation, but that the PT as an organization pushed PB adoption from above.

During the 1990s, as PB spread across the country, civil society continued to be mobilized. This was especially true in large urban areas that had large union memberships and "new social movements" (Escobar & Alvarez, 1992). Civil society organizations, especially those with a leftist-oriented ideology, sought to have more formal engagement in participatory spaces. The strong emphasis on autonomy by these movements helped situate them in a space independent of political parties but also linked to the new participatory spaces created by local governments. Over the course of the 1990s and 2000s, Brazil would build an extensive participatory architecture based on public policy management councils and public policy conferences. At the same time, PB came to represent a viable strategy for citizens and CSOs to directly participate in democratic policy-making. Thus, the pressure from civil society during the 1990s complemented leftist (and some centrist) mayors' incentives to adopt PB.

Horizontal

The spread of PB across Brazil was driven by factors commonly cited in the diffusion literature: the presence of policy networks that act as transmission belts for information, policy entrepreneurs that promote the specific policy innovation, and geographic proximity. In the case of Brazil, four distinct networks developed. First, the development of a "popular participation" network was crucial to the spread of PB across Brazil. As noted in Chap. 3, in 1993, several progressive/leftist NGOs such as IBASE, FASE, and Instituto Pólis created the National Forum for Popular Participation in Municipal Administrations (FNPP). The FNPP was independent of the Workers' Party, but also had deep ties to it. The FNPP's first two publications included short pieces written by the mayors of Porto Alegre (Tarso Genro—PT), São Paulo (Luiza Erundina—PT), Belo Horizonte (Patrus Annauis—PT), and Recife (Jarbas Vasconcelos—PMDB), by the internationally renowned educator Paulo Freire, and by NGO leaders (Silvio Caccia Bava and Pedro Pontual) (Villas Boas, 1994; Villas Boas & Telles, 1995). The FNPP played a central role in disseminating PB; the first national census of PB was carried out by the FNPP (Torres Ribeiro & Grazia, 2003). The FNPP worked with leftist governments as well as centrists, including the PMDB and PSDB, to disseminate ideas on participation, and more narrowly, PB.

A second policy network, which we label "Innovations and Good Governance," was led by social scientists in the Public Administration and Citizenship program (*Gestão Pública e Cidadanía*) at the Getúlio Vargas Foundation (FGV). The project was funded by the Ford Foundation with additional support from Brazil's National Bank for Social and Economic Development (BNDES). The program drew attention to successful subnational policy programs as a means to provide information for local governments and civil society activists. Led by Professors Marta Farah and Peter Spink, the program sponsored an annual national competition between 1996 and 2004 in which subnational governments submitted their best policies for possible selection as being among Brazil's most innovative. This program published a number of books that were geared toward showing the creative ways through which subnational governments were responding to the high demand for basic services.

PB was identified as an international "best practice" in urban management by the United Nations in 1996 at their second Habitat Conference (Porto de Oliveira, 2017, 75). In parallel, the World Bank provided funding to the municipality of Porto Alegre; part of the loan included "open" or unearmarked funds for which PB allowed citizens to prioritize public projects (World Bank Report, 2008). International awards from organizations like the United Nations and the innovations project led by the FGV carry high levels of prestige, thus conferring significant legitimacy on the government and the policy program (Peck & Theodore, 2015; Porto de Oliveira, 2017).

To account for how the presence of a Good Governance network led to the horizontal spread of PB, we draw from the FGV "Innovations" database of their Ford Foundation-sponsored Good Governance program. Wampler's statistical analysis of municipalities with over 100,000 residents shows that non-PT governments' involvement in this policy network was the strongest explanatory factor accounting for PB adoption during the 1997–2000 period (Wampler, 2008, 80). Examination of our larger dataset of more cities over the 1993–2004 period shows similar results. In the 1997–2000 period, 71% of municipalities governed by centrist or conservative mayors using PB were part of the "Innovations and Good Governance" network. During the 2001–2004 period, 57% of these municipalities with centrist and conservative mayors using PB were part of the Innovations and Good Governance network. Although we were unable to determine if these governments learned about PB through the Innovations and Good Governance network, it is clear that there is a strong correlation between the network and PB adoption by conservative and centrist parties.

In addition, two other networks developed with the express intention of promoting PB. URB-AL, sponsored by the European Union, was initiated in 2004, with Porto Alegre being the first lead city in Latin America. An initial conference in Porto Alegre drew dozens of municipal government officials and civil society activists and was followed by influential publications documenting PB's relevance for local governments (see Cabannes, 2004). Importantly, this network appears to have had a greater international effect on the dissemination of PB than it did on PB in Brazil. While Belo Horizonte followed Porto Alegre as the Brazilian host of this international organization (Porto de Oliveira, 2017), and there was likely some intra-Brazilian dissemination of information, URB-AL's primary focus appeared to be related to PB's international expansion.

In 2005, the Brazilian Network for Participatory Budgeting was founded, initially hosted by the municipal government of Belo Horizonte and then by the municipal government of Guarulhos. The network hosted workshops and acted as an information hub to expand information about PB. As we show in Fig. 1.1, in the first chapter, the decline in PB adoption was already under way when this Brazilian network was created. We infer that this network was able to slow the decline of PB as well as to promote PB in a few new municipalities, but that it wasn't able to stop the dramatic decline that would mark the 2009–2020 period.

Beyond these policy networks, we also see horizontal connections within and across leftist parties. We first find strong horizontal links between PT mayors and city- and state-level party officials (Hunter & Sugiyama, 2014, 194; Sugiyama, 2012; Villas Boas, 1994; Villas Boas & Telles, 1995). Building a grass-roots party with deep ties to social movements and unions meant that PT officials and party members spent considerable amounts of time developing inter-municipal and inter-state connections. Thus, complementing the top-down push to adopt PB (see next section), there was also considerable horizontal learning among mayors and local party officials within the PT.

Second, leftist political parties adopted PB, following the PT's lead. The five other main leftist parties adopting PB were the PSB, PDT, PV, PC do B, and PPS. Like the PT, some leaders of these parties promoted increased citizen participation in public life, greater governmental spending on public goods for poor communities, and more transparent governments. Many of these parties thus shared a general political and policy field with the Workers' Party, connecting through forums like the FNPP as well as through localized connections with the PT and social movements. In Belo Horizonte, the first PB program was adopted by a mayor from the Brazilian Socialist Party PSB) in 1993 but was part of a PSB-PT governing coalition. The PSB mayor was a medical doctor turned mayor who strongly advocated the adoption of participatory programs (Wampler, 2007, Chap. 6). In Olinda, the Communist Party of Brazil (PC do B) was elected to the Mayor's office in 2000. The incoming government had ties to its neighboring city of Recife, which was governed by the Workers' Party and had an internationally recognized and award-winning PB program.

Third, beyond leftist parties, mayors from centrist political parties (particularly the PSDB and PMDB) and conservative parties also began to adopt PB to build democratic institutions as a way of attracting voters and branding themselves as at least no less transparent and participatory than the PT. Our explanation is rooted in geography—in the comparatively rare cases that centrist and conservative parties adopted PB, it was most often where they faced competition with the PT model of local government. This meant the southern and southeastern regions of the country especially, but also state capitals and other large nearby cities in general, where institutions like PB might appeal to working-class voters because of its redistributive aims and to middle-class voters interested in reducing corruption. Of the ten cities adopting PB while under PSDB and PMDB mayors in the 1993–1996 term, seven were in the South and Southeast, and the remaining three were state capitals in the Northeast and North. In the 1997–2001 term, 21 of the 27 cases of PB adoption by center and conservative parties were in the south and southeastern parts of the country, and of the remaining six cities, three were state capitals. In the 1997–2000 term, centrist and conservative parties adopted PB in 10% of the southern and southeastern municipalities they controlled, but in only 4% of those elsewhere. In the regions where the PT was winning elections, other parties adopted PB at higher rates as well. These cities were also closer to key policy and governance networks, thus allowing information to be more quickly passed among governments across policy networks.

Recife, the state capital of Pernambuco, exemplifies this trend of centrist and/or conservative mayors learning from one another through political networks. The municipality had a long history of extensive political competition between leftist political parties and a more traditional political elite. In 1985, in the first competitive elections for mayors since 1960, Jarbas Vasconcelos was elected mayor, representing a centrist coalition (Vasconcelos' main rival was Miguel Arraes, a leftist leader who was forced into exile in 1964 by the military dictatorship when he was the state governor). Vasconcelos thus represented a moderate, centrist group that sought to deepen their ties to Recife's vibrant social movement community. Vasconcelos initiated a participatory program, "Mayor in the Neighborhood," that was largely a consultative process through which community leaders and residents presented their main demands to the mayor and his team. Vasconcelos was elected to the mayor's office again in 1992. In 1994, Vasconcelos' chief of staff and his secretary for social policy traveled to Porto Alegre to learn more about their PB process (Wampler, 2007, 225). Later that year, Vasconcelos launched a PB program largely modeled after the Porto Alegre process but maintaining an institutional design based on the "Mayor in the Neighborhood" program.

In addition to these specific networks, Porto Alegre was the first host of the World Social Forum in 2001 (and hosted again in 2002 and 2003), which brought together progressive/leftist social movements and political parties from across the world. The World Social forum served as a focal point for the person-to-person dissemination of PB; leftist activists and some public officials as well gained first-hand knowledge about Porto Alegre's PB (Goldfrank, 2012; Peck & Theodore, 2015; Porto de Oliveira, 2017). The World Social Forum thus helped trigger the spread of PB across the globe.

Vertical

During the 1990s, the Brazilian Federal system was substantially decentralized to provide additional authority, resources, and responsibilities to municipalities and states. Municipalities, for example, gained access to 15% of all public revenues and states gained access to just over 30% (Montero & Samuels, 2004). Municipalities were given the responsibility to deliver services such as basic health care, education, urban infrastructure (e.g., sanitation, street paving), and social assistance. In addition, the Brazilian federal government supported the creation of a nationwide participatory architecture based on the adoption of policy councils at three levels of government (municipal, state, federal) (Avritzer, 2009; Pires, 2011; Santos Barreto, 2011). The adoption of councils was required in five areas: education, health, social services, children and adolescents, and child protection; the federal government linked the transfer of public resources to municipalities and states to their adoption of these participatory institutions (Avritzer, 2009; Wampler et al., 2020). Although PB was not required by the federal government, the federal government created a political and policy environment that encouraged subnational governments to incorporate citizens into policymaking institutions.

In addition, fiscal decentralization marked the start of Brazil's new constitutional period (1988–1998). Municipalities gained access to new resources and responsibilities, which made PB a good policy and institutional fit for many of them. Gaining access to additional resources created an opportunity for governments to rethink how they would allocate scarce public resources. Because PB is a democratic institution that supports incremental policymaking and because there were additional resources, many governments were willing to adopt PB in order to better serve their constituents. However, toward the end of this period, by the late 1990s, and especially after the Fiscal Responsibility Law of 2000, the federal government began instituting new rules that gradually reduced subnational flexibility in allocating spending. The new rules mandated spending floors on health and education, and ceilings on personnel, as well as limits on planning long-term spending based on anticipated revenues; in effect, many local governments were forced to reduce investment spending in the early 2000s (Bezerra & Junqueira, 2018, 13). This lack of budgetary autonomy eventually made PB less appealing (see Chap. 6).

Moving beyond the federal government, political parties are also vertically integrated. In the case of Brazil, the Workers' Party stands out as the country's most vertically integrated and programmatic party (Hunter, 2010). During the 1990s, the PT didn't win many mayoral elections, but when the party won, its mayors adopted PB at a high rate (88% in 1993–1996; 93% in 1997–2000; 89% in 2001–2004).[3] The use of PB provided an excellent means through which the Workers' Party could promote the party's brand, known as the "PT way of governing" (*modo petista de governar*) (Bezerra, 2019; Bittar, 1992; Genro, 1995; Goldfrank, 2004; Hunter, 2010, 194). As Bezerra argues, "PB ended up becoming the showpiece of the *modo petista de governar* for promoting popular participation" (2019, 11). The Workers' Party was a rarity in Brazilian politics as it developed a coherent policy program, insisted on party discipline, and had a core group of committed followers (Hunter, 2010; Hunter & Sugiyama, 2014; Keck, 1992), which all helped insure high rates of PB adoption by the party's mayors. Indeed, the presence of the Workers' Party is the main factor that explains the spread of PB across Brazil; just over half of all PB programs (53%) from 1993 to 2004 are associated with the presence of the PT in either the mayor's office or the electoral coalition.

To underscore the PT's importance rather than that of the Left writ large, it is worth noting that the PT's influence was strongest when it controlled the mayor's office. For example, for the 2001–2004 period, 89% of PT-led governments adopted participatory budgeting; in this same period, only 28% of non-PT left mayors adopted PB and the PT was in the coalition for 70% of those cases. This finding reinforces the importance of the vertical influence of the Workers' Party on their local governments' decision to adopt. PB was of interest to other leftist parties, but it clearly wasn't as important to their governing and political strategies as it was to the Workers' Party.

Mayors from the PSDB and the PMDB were the second and third most frequent adopters of PB, but their party organizations didn't encourage their mayors to promote similar policies across all the cities where they governed. The PSDB was a loose confederation of local political leaders who had a significant policy and political independence (Braga et al., 2018). There was little effort by national party leaders to systematically coordinate subnational policy responses. Among PSDB-governed municipalities, 13% adopted PB in the 1997–2000 period,

[3] We thank Wendy Hunter for providing us her database on the PT. Our 1988 and 1992 election data (places where the PT captured the mayor's office) is drawn from this database. We are only analyzing cities with more than 50,000 residents.

rising slightly to 16% during the 2001–2004 period. The PMDB was similarly structured to the PSDB, with little effort by the national leadership to create a "PMDB" way of governing. The division within the PMDB is attributable to its "catch-all" nature, by which the party encompassed politicians from a wide range of ideological positions (mostly centrists, but including everything from nationalists to libertarians). Among PMDB-governed municipalities, just 3% adopted PB in 1997 and 14% in 2001. Conservative parties, particularly the PFL, began to adopt PB in higher numbers in 1997 and 2001, but the overall adoption rates were similar to the PMDB and PSDB, 4% of PFL governments adopted PB in 1997, and 13% in 2001.

Conclusion

The spread of PB across Brazil in the 1993–2004 period was driven by four processes. First, PT governments almost always adopted PB. Thus, winning mayoral elections was crucial showing the vital importance of internal (municipal-level) politics. But it also included vertical processes, whereby the PT strongly encouraged all PT municipal governments to adopt PB. Horizontal processes were also important because PT governments were linked to each other. Quite simply, the PT was at the center of the spread of PB, accounting for 53% of all cases adopted between 1993 and 2004 either through its mayors or through its leftist coalition partners.

Second, horizontal policy networks also help us to understand why non-PT governments adopted PB. We find four policy networks (FNPP, FGV, URB-AL, RBOP) that promoted the adoption of PB. Among centrist and conservative governments, their involvement in a national "Innovations in Good Governance" network (sponsored by FGV) was the strongest factor to explain why they adopted PB. Relatedly, the PT's most significant political rivals located in the political center (PSDB and PMDB) adopted the majority of the new PB cases that weren't associated with the PT or the left. Importantly, it was only a minority of PMDB and PSDB governments that adopted PB, suggesting that PB wasn't part of a coordinated national strategy on the part of these parties but rather due to the political motivations of individual mayors as they surveyed their local competitors as well as potential local government models.

Many of the governments adopting PB were doing so in the hope that it would improve social, political, governance well-being. During the spread of PB, there was limited evidence that clearly demonstrated PB's impact, which meant that much of the governments' commitment to PB was based on ideology and political calculations, as well as the signals sent through their policy and political networks. We turn, in the next chapter, to an overview of the outcomes that researchers were able to identify in order to better understand the results that mayors sensed PB might produce.

References

Avritzer, L. (2002). *Democracy and the Public Space in Latin America*. Princeton University Press.

Avritzer, L. (2009). *Participatory Institutions in Democratic Brazil*. Woodrow Wilson Center.

Baiocchi, G., & Ganuza, E. (2017). *Popular Democracy: The Paradox of Participation*. Stanford University Press.

Baiocchi, G., Heller, P., & Silva, S. (2011). *Bootstrapping Democracy: Transforming Local Governance and Civil Society in Brazil*. Stanford University Press.

Bezerra, C. (2016). *Por que o Orçamento Participativo entrou em declínio no Brasil. Mudanças na legislação fiscal e seu impacto sobre a estratégia partidária*. VII Seminário Discente da Pós-Graduação em Ciência Política da USP.

Bezerra, C. (2019). Os sentidos da participação para o Partido dos Trabalhadores (1980–2016). *Revista Brasileira de Ciência Sociais, 34*(100), e3410016. https://doi.org/10.1590/3410016/2019

Bezerra, C., & Junqueira, M. (2018). *Why Has Participatory Budgeting Adoption Declined in Brazil?* 114th Annual Meeting of the American Political Science Association. Boston, Massachusetts.

Bittar, J. (1992). *O modo petista de governar*. Camargo Soares.

Braga, M., Costa, V., & Fernandes, J. (2018). Dinâmicas de funcionamento e controle do poder nos partidos políticos: os casos do PT e PSDB no estado de São Paulo. *Revista Brasileira de Ciências Sociais, 33*(96), e339614. https://doi.org/10.17666/339614/2018

Cabannes, Y. (2004). Participatory Budgeting: A Significant Contribution to Participatory Democracy. *Environment and Urbanization, 16*(1), 27–46.

Eaton, K., & Dickovick, T. (2004). The Politics of Re-centralization in Argentina and Brazil. *Latin American Research Review, 39*(1), 90–122.

Escobar, A., & Alvarez, S. (Eds.). (1992). *The Making of Social Movements in Latin America*. Westview Press.

Genro, T. (1995). *Utopia Possível* (2nd ed.). Artes e Ofícios Goldfrank 2004.

Goldfrank, B. (2004). Conclusion: The End of Politics or a New Beginning for the Left? In Chavez, D. & Goldfrank, B. (Eds.), *The Left in the City*. Latin American Bureau and Transnational Institute.
Goldfrank, B. (2012). The World Bank and the Globalization of Participatory Budgeting. *Journal of Public Deliberation, 8*(2), 7.
Hunter, W. (2010). *The Transformation of the Workers' Party in Brazil, 1989–2009*. Cambridge University Press.
Hunter, W., & Sugiyama, N. B. (2014). Transforming Subjects into Citizens: Insights from Brazil's Bolsa Família. *Perspectives on Politics, 12*(4), 829–845.
Keck, M. E. (1992). *The Workers' Party and Democratization in Brazil*. Yale University Press.
Lüchman, L., Romão, W., & Borba, J. (2018). 30 Years of Participatory Budgeting in Brazil: The Lessons Learned. In N. Días (Ed.), *Hope for Democracy: 30 Years of Participatory Budgeting Worldwide* (pp. 89–103). Oficina.
Mainwaring, S., & Scully, T. (1995). *Building Democratic Institutions: Party Systems in Latin America*. Stanford University Press.
Montero, A. P., & Samuels, D. J. (2004). *Decentralization and Democracy in Latin America*. University of Notre Dame Press.
Peck, J., & Theodore, N. (2015). *Fast Policy: Experimental Statecraft at the Thresholds of Neoliberalism*. University of Minnesota Press.
Pires, R. (2011). *Efetividade das instituições participativas no Brasil: estratégias de avaliação*. IPEA.
Porto de Oliveira, O. (2017). *International Policy Diffusion and Participatory Budgeting: Ambassadors of Participation, International Institutions and Transnational Networks*. Palgrave Macmillan.
Santos Barreto, D. (2011). Pesquisa de Informacoes Basicas. In R. Pires (Ed.), *Efetividade das Instituições Participativas no Brasil: Estratégias de Avaliação*. IPEA.
Spada, P. (2014). *The Diffusion of Participatory Governance Innovations: A Panel Data Analysis of the Adoption and Survival of Participatory Budgeting in Brazil*. Annual Conference of the Latin American Studies Association.
Sugiyama, N. B. (2012). *Diffusion of Good Government: Social Sector Reforms in Brazil*. University of Notre Dame Press.
Tendler, J. (1997). *Good Government in the Tropics*. Johns Hopkins University Press.
Torres Ribeiro, A., & Grazia, G. (2003). *Experiência de Orçamento Participativo no Brasil: Periodo de 1997 a 2000*. Editora Vozes.
Villas Boas, R. (1994). *Participação Popular nos Governos Locais*. Instituto Pólis.
Villas Boas, R., & Telles, V. (1995). *Poder Local, Participação Popular, Construção da Cidadania*. Fórum Nacional de Participação Popular nas Administrações Municipais.
Wampler, B. (2007). *Participatory Budgeting in Brazil: Contestation, Cooperation, and Accountability*. Pennsylvania State University Press.

Wampler, B. (2008). When Does Participatory Democracy Deepen the Quality of Democracy? Lessons from Brazil. *Comparative Politics, 41*(1), 61–81.
Wampler, B. (2009). Following in the Footsteps of Policy Entrepreneurs: Policy Advocates and Pro Forma Adopters. *Journal of Development Studies, 45*(4), 572–592.
Wampler, B., McNulty, S., & Touchton, M. (2021). *Participatory Budgeting in Global Perspective*. Oxford University Press.
Wampler, B., Sugiyama, N. B., & Touchton, M. (2020). *Democracy at Work: Pathways to Well-Being in Brazil*. Cambridge University Press.
World Bank Report. (2008). *Brazil: Toward a More Inclusive and Effective Participatory Budget in Porto Alegre (Report No. 40144-BR)*. World Bank.

CHAPTER 5

Outcomes: When and Where Did PB Live Up to the Hype?

Abstract Governments, political parties, civil society organizations, and international organizations promoting participatory budgeting have long looked for evidence that might support their political and policy campaigns that PB would deepen democracy and transform lives. In this chapter, we turn our attention to analyzing research findings on PB outcomes with regard to five key areas: Democracy, civil society, governance and accountability, public goods distribution, and well-being. We identify a range of positive outcomes generated associated with the adoption of PB, yet we also show how many of these results are highly localized (building sewage lines in a single *favela*), small-scale but of great importance to specific neighborhoods (e.g., street paving), or incremental in nature (e.g., reforming a local health clinic).

Keywords Participatory budgeting • Brazil • Porto Alegre • Belo Horizonte • Democracy • Civil society • Accountability • Public goods • Well-being

Politicians and civil society activists looking to promote the adoption of PB often did so in the hopes that it would improve a wide range of outcomes: deepen the quality of democracy, strengthen civil society, improve governance, and promote equity and social justice. A tall order, to be sure.

B. Wampler, B. Goldfrank, *The Rise, Spread, and Decline of Brazil's Participatory Budgeting*,
https://doi.org/10.1007/978-3-030-90058-8_5

To what extent were researchers able to confirm any of these outcomes? Was there any solid evidence of PB programs producing this type of change? In this chapter, we identify a range of positive outcomes generated associated with the adoption of PB; as we show in this chapter, many of these positive changes are more likely to be present in the earlier cases of PB (during PB's creation and spread phases) as well as among municipalities that kept PB going for at least eight years. Broadly, the overall body of evidence shows that PB was frequently associated with changing state-society relations, with increasing the number of civil society organizations, and with improving accountability and equity in public service provision (Abers, 2000; Avritzer, 2002; Baiocchi, 2005; Baiocchi et al., 2011; Fedozzi, 1997; Goldfrank, 2011; Marquetti, 2003; Marquetti et al., 2008; Wampler, 2007, 2015).

However, we also identify how many of these results are highly localized (building sewage lines in a single *favela*), small-scale but of great importance to specific neighborhoods (e.g., street paving), or incremental in nature (e.g., reforming a local health clinic). Quite simply, many PB projects are relatively small, which limits their potential impact on the overall health and well-being of an entire city. Of course, there are exceptions, as we find evidence of housing projects and major sewage projects being selected through PB (World Bank, 2008). But these large projects are the exceptions that reinforce the general rule that most PB programs focus on small infrastructure projects (see Cabannes, 2004). In this chapter, we argue that participants and non-participating citizens may be able to connect specific infrastructure projects with PB, but it is difficult for them to understand how these projects are associated with broader changes in governance, civil society, or well-being. As a result, governments operating in a competitive electoral environment find it more difficult to actively support a program that doesn't necessarily provide strong electoral pay-offs.

Finally, we note that there is an unevenness across PB programs—some programs provide robust results while others generate negative outcomes. Thus, we need to be clear that some PB programs function quite poorly, which leads citizens to believe that they hold little power and that the adoption of PB was for "show" as part of a "white-washing" project. Of course, there is a long-standing fear among civil society activists in Brazil, and across the world, that government leaders will adopt participatory programs as part of an effort to demonstrate that the government is inclusionary, participatory, and transparent, but that the programs won't delegate any real authority or resources to citizens. In these cases, activists worry that PB (and similar programs) are "dog and pony" events that generate short-term support for the government but don't necessarily generate social and political change.

Governments, parties, civil society organizations, and international organizations promoting PB have long looked for evidence that might support their political and policy campaigns that PB would deepen democracy and transform lives. To illustrate the interest in demonstrating how PB affects outcomes, we turn to field work conducted in 1999 by then PhD student Brian Wampler, who was living in Porto Alegre to carry out dissertation research. He attended a PB meeting and budget workshop in the southern city of Porto Alegre; several hundred people were in attendance at the PB meeting and a group of around 30 were in attendance at the budget workshop. In both meetings, with different levels of detail, government officials argued that the adoption of PB led to an increase in the municipal-level Human Development Index (HDI-M), thus greatly improving people's lives. The Human Development Index, inspired by the work of Nobel-prize winning economist Dr. Amartya Sen, incorporates three basic components—life expectancy, education (adult literacy and gross education enrollment), and gross domestic product per capita—to try to provide a more comprehensive understanding of a country's overall health. Brazil is one of the few countries in the Global South that collects this data at the municipal level (HDI-M).

The government official in Porto Alegre provided data to show that the HDI-M in Porto Alegre dramatically improved between 1991 (roughly, when PB started) and 1999. The government officials made a compelling argument, in both meetings, that it was the decisions made by citizens through the PB that drove this improvement. The officials cited the types of public works projects selected by citizens—water and sewer lines, building health care clinics, and reforming schools—as well as the income generated for local residents by hiring local firms to implement these projects. Over the next couple of days, Wampler reviewed the HDI-M data for all large Brazilian municipalities. At first glance, the government official's story was accurate—Porto Alegre's HDI-M had improved drastically. But then Wampler noticed something else in the data—similarly situated municipalities without PB had similar increases in their HDI-M, suggesting that PB may not have been the only factor causing the improvement in the municipality.[1]

[1]We note that Ribas Vargas (2007) found statistically significant association between the adoption of PB and an increase in the HDI-M between 1991 and 2000. She finds that "municipalities with PB tend to reach better scores on human development more rapidly than those that did not implement PB" (p. 74, our translation). The principal limitation to

At a different moment in 1999, also in the city of Porto Alegre, Wampler was attending a PB meeting with several hundred participants. Wampler had been attending meetings for several months in an effort to better understand the process. Prior to the meeting's official start, Wampler and a participant were talking about PB, Porto Alegre, and Brazil more broadly. The participant asked him a question that would help to inform Wampler's research trajectory. She asked: Will our participation in PB make a difference in our lives? She then talked about the time and energy that she and her fellow community members were spending on the process. She was uncertain if PB would be "transformative." This question and line of inquiry is understandable anywhere, but perhaps especially in a socio-political context in which Brazilian citizens, especially poor citizens, have very low levels of trust. Thus, her question can be interpreted quite narrowly—will this elected government follow through and implement the public work projects that we selected? But her question is also much broader because it taps into whether a local democratic institution can go beyond immediate, concrete, incremental improvements to be transformative in the long term.

In this chapter, we turn our attention to how researchers have tried to answer her question by addressing findings in five key areas: democracy, civil society, governance and accountability, public goods distribution, and well-being outcomes. We selected these themes because PB's advocates believed that PB would be transformative in these different areas as well as because this is where researchers carried out the most interesting, compelling studies.

Democracy

PB is a democratic institution designed to move beyond the confines of representative democracy by allowing citizens to be directly involved in making government decision-making processes. As Brazil transitioned into a new democratic regime, more radical democrats worried that the organizational and upper-class bias associated with representative democracy would not permit the new democratic regime to address the social, political, and civil needs of the majority (Ross, 2006; Santos, 1998;

this excellent MA thesis was the limited number of control variables, making it difficult to assess the extent to which it was PB or other factors that might be affecting change (which is true of the World Bank (2008) study as well).

Schattschneider, 1960). Brazil, of course, was and continues to be one of the most unequal countries in the world, with large numbers of urban Brazilians in *favelas* and lacking basic access to sewage, electricity, water, as well as public goods like education and health care. "Democratizing democracy" was thus a process of changing the basic power dynamics of a society to ensure the incorporation of non-elite actors in key decision-making venues (Santos, 2005).

Early research conducted on PB's democratizing potential largely focused on the most well-known cases of PB: the cities of Porto Alegre and Belo Horizonte. The methodological approach generally employed consists of a single case study that involves a "deep dive" into the local political and social contexts. Elite interviews, focus groups, participant-observation, participant surveys, and institutional analysis are key methods used to collect data. Many of the key scholarly works in this area seek to provide a comprehensive analysis of change by situating the specific program, PB, in its broader local context.

Boaventura Santos (1998, 2005) identified PB's democratizing potential, arguing that PB had the potential to "democratize democracy" by expanding the breadth of who participates, the location of where decisions are made, and the type of decisions that citizens can make. Santos recognized PB as an effort to move beyond the confines of representative democracy by expanding the *demos*—those who can actively participate in formal public institutions. The empirical evidence collected over nearly 30 years of research demonstrates that the majority of PB participants were poor citizens with average levels of income and education (Abers, 1998, 2000; Baiocchi, 2005; Baiocchi et al., 2011; Cidade, 2003; Nylen, 2002, 2003; Wampler, 2007, 2015). In this way, we can confirm that PB contributed to changing the socio economic status of who was involved in policy decision-making.

In addition, rich ethnographic work by scholars such as Gianpaolo Baiocchi, Rebecca Abers, Leonardo Avritzer, and Claudia Faria show that these same citizens were working to build their communities and that they were also involved in making binding decisions that directed the government and its administrative apparatus to implement specific types of programs. In the well-known cases in Brazil, such as Porto Alegre and Belo Horizonte, there is clear evidence that poor citizens, mostly from favelas, were able to deliberate in public, which was then followed by a public vote through which the interested citizens selected projects.

Although the inclusion of poor citizens into PB was an important step, we note that most PB programs involve a small part of the budget. Most PB programs focus on the "investment" budget, which consists of spending on new infrastructure projects. During the early 1990s, when PB programs were getting going, the investment portion was typically around 10% of the overall budget (in some cases, it was upward of 15%). Governments then had to decide what portion of the budget they would provide for deliberation, with the most strongly committed governments providing nearly 100% of the investment budget (Wampler, 2007, Chapter 4). However, between 85% and 98% of the overall budget was not available for deliberation through PB. In Brazil, as in most other government budgets, the largest budget expenditure is for personnel—paying civil servants to carry out the administrative functions of the state. Most budget-related issues were not included in PB, thus limiting the broader democratic potential of PB. In sum, we can confirm that most PB programs were inclusive but that their inclusion was limited to a relatively small (but often meaningful) portion of the budget.

We note that there are a couple of major research-oriented shortcomings that make it difficult to boldly and conclusively declare that PB helped to "democratize democracy" in terms of individuals. First, there are no comparative surveys or studies that compare the attitudes and behaviors of participants and non-participants. This means we don't know if the democratizing elements were limited to the PB meetings themselves or if there was a "spill-over" into the broader community. Second, there are no "pre-test" and "post-test" surveys of participants. In this type of approach, researchers would gather information on a participant's attitudes and behaviors prior to their participation. There would then be another survey administered at the end of the participatory experience to identify if there were any changes in their attitudes and behaviors. Unfortunately, we have no surveys that used a pre- and post-test approach, which means that we cannot really know the extent to which participants' attitudes and behaviors changed. It is entirely possible that citizens came into PB with more democratic attitudes and behaviors; in this case, PB would have a weaker effect than preexisting and complementary activities that take place outside of PB.

Civil Society

Broadly, empirical work on civil society and PB includes two distinct lines of analysis: a "political culture" approach whereby researchers sought to better understand if and how PB alters how citizens and CSOs organize themselves, engage in public venues, and interact with public officials; a "density" approach whereby researchers sought to better understand if and how PB contributed to an increase in the number of civil society organizations. The general theoretical proposition is that PB would stimulate people to join community organizations and social movements in order to work more effectively within PB. We begin with the political culture approach.

Leonardo Avritzer focused on how the development of a new type of civil society helped to set the basic conditions that would permit the expansion of new participatory institutions in Brazil. Avritzer (2002) argues that the creation of "participatory publics" within civil society generated new forms of engagement; citizens learned how to practice democracy by deliberating and voting within local community-based CSOs. When PB was developed, these skills were then further honed in the formal PB meetings as well as in community meetings (Avritzer, 2002). Thus, PB helped citizens develop skills that are often necessary to engaging in democratic politics—community organization and mobilization, deliberation, negotiation, promoting interests in public venues.

Research by others demonstrate how the political culture of Porto Alegre's neighborhood associations changed from a more presidentialist, top-down style to a more participatory, bottom-up style as a result of PB. Rebecca Abers (2000, 220–221) found that a key way in which PB attracted participants and revitalized civic life in Porto Alegre was by focusing on the immediate needs of specific communities. In the districts she studied most intensely, Abers (2000, 161–166) found an increase in the holding of elections and regular meetings in the neighborhood associations involved in PB; Baiocchi (2001, 55; 2002, 49, 83) discovered the same pattern. Goldfrank's (2011, Chap. 6) interviewees in 1998 and 1999 with budget councilors in various districts throughout the city similarly indicated that PB had a direct effect on the democratization of neighborhood associations and in many cases led to district-wide confederations. Many of the budget councilors interviewed had never been socially or politically active in their neighborhoods but began starting new associations or democratizing existing ones after attending PB meetings. William

Nylen (2003) discovered that PB councilors often revived moribund neighborhood associations in the cities of Belo Horizonte and Betim as well.

Several early scholars of PB focused on its informal educational benefits for civil society activists. Baiocchi (2005), for example, argues that PB in Porto Alegre acted as a "school of democracy" whereby citizens and CSOs developed democratic skills. Nylen (2003, Chapter 6) also sees PB as a school of democracy in Belo Horizonte and Betim, and demonstrates that, while PB in those cities mostly mobilized those already active in their communities, it contributed to their expanding their civic and political engagement. Coming from the Freireian tradition of popular education, Daniel Schugurensky (2006) presents PB in Porto Alegre as an "informal school of citizenship," showing how community activists gained civic and political knowledge, skills, and attitudes through participating in PB.

Finally, Baiocchi et al. (2011) find that PB deepens democracy when civil society organizations can organize independently and develop their own demands. Their work shows that a deep understanding of the nature of civil society before PB is implemented is the best way to conceive of the potential for results. This finding also suggests that in some cases with extremely weak civil society sectors, reform efforts may be more productive if focused on other aspects of democracy, and not PB. As Baiocchi et al. (2011) write, "local context was critical to shaping outcomes" (145).

Numerous studies demonstrate that the adoption of PB was associated with an increase in the number of CSOs. Baiocchi (2002, Table 3) found, for example, that Porto Alegre's active neighborhood associations increased from roughly 300 in 1988 to about 540 in 1998, while Goldfrank (2011, 244) found 664 associations registered with the Community Relations Office as of 2001. Interestingly, Baiocchi's (2001, 56–58) correlational analysis also shows that it was in the city's poorest districts—precisely where participation rates in PB were highest—that associational density grew the most.

In a similar vein, Touchton and Wampler (2014) find that municipalities with PB have greater numbers of CSOs in comparison to municipalities without PB. We are able to show that the adoption of PB led to an increase in the number of CSOs. Why? It is largely because PB rewards group mobilization. The voting process is typically based on the number of votes cast for a project; voters vote for several projects and the projects with the most votes would be selected for inclusion into the annual budget. Thus, individual participants or small groups would be less likely to secure enough votes for their projects, thus ensuring defeat. Larger groups are more likely to secure their preferred projects because they turn out their followers in greater numbers (See also Goldfrank, 2011, Chapter 6). In many ways, this voting system mirrors representative democracy, which rewards well-organized groups. The principal difference from representative democracy is that many PB programs used "social justice" rules that encouraged the direct participation of poor citizens.

However, we also see that many PB programs don't necessarily engage in "best practices" when it comes to civil society and democratic processes. Navarro (2003) worried that Porto Alegre's PB program was generating a form of participatory clientelism, whereby community groups were "captured" by the municipal government. In his analysis, Navarro argued that PB eroded the political autonomy of community groups because the only way for them to secure resources was to mobilize themselves through the PB process, which the Workers' Party administered. If the Workers' Party were to lose office, it would be less likely that future governments would implement projects selected through PB.

Ben Junge's research on civil society in Porto Alegre later in the 2000s demonstrates that PB generated considerable discord among civil society organizations. The intense competition through PB made it more difficult for community groups to generate the types of social unity and solidarity that early PB proponents hoped for (Junge, 2018). Rather than being a positive-sum relationship in which inter-group collaboration rewarded most organizations, PB began to be seen as a zero-sum relationship in which projects selected for implementation in some communities meant that other communities wouldn't receive funding.

Governance and Accountability

Rebecca Abers' work on PB jump-started the conversation in the English-language academic world. Abers' important early article (1998) and her book (2000) demonstrated how PB was altering the distribution of resources and political power in Porto Alegre. Importantly, Abers demonstrates that PB's focus on localized need and immediate project implementation made PB a key locus of political power. Citizens had an incentive to be involved in PB because it was where resources were distributed.

Wampler's (2007) book analyzed PB through the lens of accountability. This work was the first to employ a medium-N analysis. In his comparison of eight cities, Wampler found that two of the cases of PB (Porto

Alegre and Ipatinga) demonstrated consistently positive outcomes; PB helped to generate improvements in vertical, horizontal, and social accountability. But Wampler also found that the cities of Blumenau and Rio Claro produced very weak results. The governments and CSOs in both municipalities were only partially invested in supporting PB.

Four additional cities (São Paolo, Belo Horizonte, Recife, and Santo André) produced mixed results, meaning that their programs produced positive outcomes in some areas but produced weak or even negative effects in other areas. Wampler argues that identifying the government's political incentives as well as CSOs' willingness to both partner with and contest the government offers the strongest explanation for outcomes. The broader point for our analysis is that there was significant variation regarding the extent to which PB programs were able to produce robust impacts; when governments invested extensive political and financial capital into PB, there was then a greater likelihood that they would produce significant change. Mixed outcomes were much more likely, which helps to explain why other governments were increasingly reluctant to use PB.

Touchton et al. (2020) analyze the extent to which the presence of PB is associated with greater changes in a local government's revenue collection. In Brazil, the overwhelming majority of municipal budgets come from fiscal transfers from the national and state governments; for most municipalities between 90% and 100% of their budget comes from these transfers. Municipal governments raise local revenues through property and sales taxes to provide additional revenues to support government policies. We find that governments adopting PB collect nearly 40% more in local tax revenues than comparable municipalities without PB. These additional revenues collected were roughly equivalent to the municipalities' "discretionary" resources, which is where the funding for most PB project comes from. In other words, local government collected additional tax revenues to cover the additional spending associated with PB. Governments are incentivized to collect additional revenues because they need the revenues to implement the projects selected by citizens. In addition, we also assert that these PB-adopting municipalities might have also benefited from an improvement in citizens' "tax morale." By this, we suggest that a change in citizens' attitudes may have encouraged more of them to become regular taxpayers.

Similarly, Schneider and Baquero (2006) find that government officials in Porto Alegre built up the city government's administrative capacity to ensure that they would capture more of the taxes already on the books.

Schneider and Baquero draw on interviews with government and civil society sources and a public opinion survey to argue that people were more willing to pay their taxes because public goods were being provided through PB. There was both a change in government activity (governments collecting taxes already on the books) and an apparent improvement in "tax morale," whereby citizens are more willing to pay taxes because they believed that the government was investing in projects selected through PB.

There is also a substantial body of evidence from Brazil indicating that better-performing PB programs improve accountability (Abers, 2000; Avritzer, 2002, 2009; Baiocchi et al., 2011; Wampler, 2007, 2015). New relationships can emerge that are less adversarial and more collaborative when states and society work together more effectively (Montambeault, 2019). This finding is echoed by Baiocchi et al.'s (2011) comparison of four PB processes to four comparable cites without PB in Brazil. In the PB cases, CSOs were able to effectively hold elected officials to account, especially in areas with relatively strong civil society sectors before PB was introduced.

However, many governments with PB programs are unwilling or unable to invest the necessary resources or administrative support to make the programs work well, which limits the extent to which they are able to affect governance (Montambeault, 2016; Navarro, 2003; Romão, 2011; Wampler, 2007). The governments are unwilling to invest resources because there are weak political incentives for them to dedicate their limited political or financial capital into the project. These governments were often induced by the national party (e.g., Workers' Party) (vertical considerations), by intra-party bargaining (e.g., majority group vs. democratic socialists in the Workers' Party), or by inter-party bargaining (e.g., Workers' Party in minority position in government). In these types of cases, the promotion of PB wasn't the primary political objective of the government, which led them to provide only partial support. Because PB is a relatively time-intensive participatory program, lukewarm support from an incumbent government was often sufficient to undermine the program. How might this "undermining" of a participatory program take place?

Governments might undermine a PB program by providing more limited administrative staff to support the program. This staff struggles to advertise the meetings, thus reducing the number of participants. The staff struggles to prepare the necessary information on budgets and projects—information that is vital to allow citizens to make informed choices. Importantly, the government doesn't provide sufficient resources to implement projects, nor does it strongly encourage different government agencies to reorganize their bureaucracies to get things done. When PB programs lack the strong support of the government, PB programs tend to wither away—death by a thousand cuts.

Public Goods Distribution

PB programs were initially designed to expand citizens' and communities' access to public goods. PB's advocates hoped that PB would result in an increase in public goods distribution and service delivery in poor communities. In the late 1980s and 1990s, many urban shantytowns (*favelas* or *vilas*) lacked basic infrastructure such as water and sewage infrastructure, electricity, paved roads, local health clinics, and local service centers.

Adelmir Marquetti, an economist working in Porto Alegre, was the first researcher to clearly identify a relationship between public spending and communities' wealth. Marquetti focuses on the Porto Alegre PB program. He found that Porto Alegre's PB programs spent a greater percentage of resources on a per capita basis in those communities where residents had a lower standard of living (2003). Marquetti's work was the first to definitively show that PB programs were allocating greater resources to those communities with greater need. This finding was important because it confirmed what PB's advocates often claimed: PB was an institution that successfully managed to allocate greater resources to poor communities. Pires (2008) used a similar methodology to examine the case of Belo Horizonte and found that there, too, poor communities that had less public infrastructure were allocated a greater level of resources on a per capita basis. Wampler (2015) expanded Pires' work in Belo Horizonte, demonstrating similar outcomes.

Researchers from the World Bank (2008) focusing on Porto Alegre found that PB led to improved access to water services, which improves citizens' daily lives and can also have a broader effect on health due to improved sanitation. This preliminary evidence provided support for the assertion that PB could help to improve well-being, often through redistribution of resources to poor communities (Goldfrank, 2011; Goldfrank & Schneider, 2006; Marquetti et al., 2008). In addition, Boulding and Wampler (2010) employed a cross-municipal analysis to show that PB programs were associated with increased spending on health care and sanitation. This was the first large-N comparative study to demonstrate that a wide range of PB municipalities was allocating resources differently than municipalities that didn't adopt PB. The shift to spending on health and sanitation is important because these are services for which poor citizens largely depend on public provision.

Overall, researchers have documented that PB programs are associated with changes in how municipal governments distribute public resources. When analyzing spending across cities, research on Porto Alegre and Belo Horizonte clearly demonstrates that these programs spent greater resources, on a per capita basis, in poorer communities than in wealthier communities. Unfortunately, we just don't know if these findings are generalizable to other PB programs. Nonetheless, when we compare municipal budgets in PB and non-PB cities, several studies show that PB governments spent more on health, sanitation, and education, thus demonstrating that the adoption of PB is associated with greater spending on budget items of particular importance to poor individuals and communities.

Well-Being

The final area of research concerns the potential impact on well-being. Researchers wanted to know if the presence of PB is associated with improvements in well-being, such as greater access to public education, improvements in the quality of public education, or infant or maternal mortality. Gonçalves (2014) and Touchton and Wampler (2014) identify improvements in citizens' well-being (see also Boulding & Wampler, 2010; Touchton et al., 2017). With data spanning 20 years, Touchton and Wampler (2014) find that PB programs are strongly associated with greater municipal spending on health care and sanitation and lower infant mortality. The effect is greater in programs that have been in place longer and where Workers' Party mayors are in power. There is no consensus on how long it may take for effects on well-being to appear, but initial work suggests that reductions in infant mortality can happen over a relatively short time (Gonçalves, 2014; Touchton & Wampler, 2014). Thus, one key implication is that it is better to adopt PB than not to adopt because PB is associated with improvements in a key health and development indicator.

More recently, Wampler and Touchton (2019) compared municipalities with PB programs. They find that those PB programs with an explicit set of "social justice" rules are associated with improvements in a key area of social well-being: infant mortality. They argue that the presence of these specific rules—most notably, an internal rule that guaranteed poorer communities a greater percentage of resources on a per capita basis—contributed to an increase in public health-related spending in poor communities. This is associated with a decrease in infant mortality because young women would have an easier time accessing pre-natal care. This finding suggests that the first step of implementing PB is important but that a second step—adopting an institutional design that promotes the interests of low-income communities—will produce even better results.

In sum, the evidence that PB programs are associated with improvements in well-being is somewhat thin. We have three large-N studies that demonstrate that PB is associated with important material changes in people's lives. We also note that the causal arrow between PB and a key indicator (infant mortality) is not direct. That is, while we can identify how internal causal processes within PB might affect infant mortality (e.g., citizens vote to invest in reforming health clinics or for greater sanitation), a change in governance, and health governance more specifically, might be necessary to induce the policy and administrative reforms that help to reduce infant mortality. In other words, PB is best understood as one part of a larger effort to improve basic health outcomes.

Conclusion

Overall, this chapter identifies a broad body of evidence that demonstrates that many PB programs were able to produce positive social and political change. The single-case study work, largely in the cities of Porto Alegre and Belo Horizonte, helped to generate theory on how PB was generating this change. Following the expansion of theoretical concepts used to explain PB, a series of small-N and medium-N analyses found compelling evidence that PB was, in fact, generating positive social change, as PB proponents hoped that it would, though not in all cases.

There are a couple of lessons that we draw from this study and the broader debate. First, it was better for Brazilian citizens to live in a municipality that adopted PB than somewhere that did not adopt PB. Second, it was even better for citizens' well-being if their PB program adopted specific social justice rules than if it did not adopt them. More broadly, a key lesson is that institutional design has an important impact on outcomes. In other words, having PB was a net positive for cities, but having a specific type of PB generated greater improvements for citizens.

However, not all PB programs produce positive results, nor were the outcomes consistent across the broader universe of PB cases. Many PB programs were not strongly supported by governments or civil society, thus leading to relatively weak cases. In the worst-case scenario, we can assert that PB programs may have negative impacts—an increase in cynicism and a decrease in trust because governments fail to hold robust meetings and/or fail to implement projects selected by citizens.

Interestingly, most of the evidence using medium or large-N studies to assess associated impacts began to be published in the early to mid-2000s, with the bulk of the publications occurring after 2007. Thus, during the first decade of PB (1989–2000), governments weren't adopting PB based on evidence but were adopting PB based on the hope that it would generate positive social and political outcomes. In other words, the commitment of PB was based on ideological or hopeful interpretations of what PB might be able to generate. Mayors and policymakers might have sometimes intuitively understood that PB was generating positive change, but they had limited concrete evidence to support this belief. By the time that researchers began to demonstrate that PB in Brazil was associated with positive social change, PB was already on the decline. In the next chapter, we turn our attention to the issue of why fewer and fewer municipal governments were adopting this democratic innovation.

References

Abers, R. (1998). From Clientelism to Cooperation: Local Government, Participatory Policy, and Civic Organizing in Porto Alegre, Brazil. *Politics and Society, 26*(4), 511–537.

Abers, R. (2000). *Inventing Local Democracy: Grassroots Politics in Brazil.* Lynne Rienner.

Avritzer, L. (2002). *Democracy and the Public Space in Latin America.* Princeton University Press.

Avritzer, L. (2009). *Participatory Institutions in Democratic Brazil.* Woodrow Wilson Center.

Baiocchi, G. (2001). Participation, Activism, and Politics: The Porto Alegre Experiment and Deliberative Democratic Theory. *Politics and Society, 29*(1), 43–72.

Baiocchi, G. (2002). Synergizing Civil Society: State-Civil Society Regimes in Porto Alegre, Brazil. *Political Power and Social Theory, 15*, 3–86.

Baiocchi, G. (2005). *Militants and Citizens: The Politics of Participatory Democracy in Porto Alegre*. Stanford University Press.

Baiocchi, G., Heller, P., & Silva, S. (2011). *Bootstrapping Democracy: Transforming Local Governance and Civil Society in Brazil*. Stanford University Press.

Boulding, C., & Wampler, B. (2010). Voice, Votes, and Resources: Evaluating the Effect of Participatory Democracy on Well-being. *World Development, 38*(1), 125–135.

Cabannes, Y. (2004). Participatory Budgeting: A Significant Contribution to Participatory democracy. *Environment and Urbanization, 16*(1), 27–46.

CIDADE. (2003). *Who Is the Public of the Participatory Budgeting? 2002*. CIDADE.

Fedozzi, L. (1997). *Orçamento Participativo: Reflexões Sobre a Experiência de Porto Alegre*. Tomo Editorial.

Goldfrank, B. (2011). *Deepening Local Democracy in Latin America: Participation, Decentralization, and the Left*. Pennsylvania State University Press.

Goldfrank, B., & Schneider, A. (2006). Competitive Institution Building: The PT and Participatory Budgeting in Rio Grande do Sul. *Latin American Politics & Society, 48*(3), 1–31.

Gonçalves, S. (2014). The Effects of Participatory Budgeting on Municipal Expenditures and Infant Mortality in Brazil. *World Development, 53*, 94–110.

Junge, B. (2018). *Cynical Citizenship: Gender, Regionalism, and Political Subjectivity in Porto Alegre*. University of New Mexico Press.

Marquetti, A. (2003). Democracia, Equidade e Effciencia, o Caso do Orçamento Participativo em Porto Alegre. In L. Avritzer & Z. Navarro (Eds.), *A Inovação Democrática no Brasil: O Orçamento Participativo* (pp. 129–156). Cortez Editores.

Marquetti, A., Campos, G., & Pires, R. (2008). *Democracia participativa e redistribuição:análise de experiências de orçamento participativo*. Xamã.

Montambeault, F. (2016). Participatory Citizenship in the Making? The Multiple Citizenship Trajectories of Participatory Budgeting Participants in Brazil. *Journal of Civil Society, 12*(3), 282–298.

Montambeault, F. (2019). It Was Once a Radical Democratic Proposal: Theories of Gradual Institutional Change in Brazilian Participatory Budgeting. *Latin American Politics and Society, 61*(1), 29–53.

Navarro, Z. (2003). O "Orçamento Participativo" de Porto Alegre (1989-2002): um conciso comentário crítico. In L. Avritzer & Z. Navarro (Eds.), *A Inovação Democratica no Brasil* (pp. 89–128). Cortez Editores.

Nylen, W. (2002). Testing the Empowerment Thesis: The Participatory Budget in Belo Horizonte & Betim, Brazil. *Comparative Politics, 34*(2), 127–145.

Nylen, W. (2003). *Participatory Democracy Versus Elitist Democracy: Lessons from Brazil*. Palgrave Macmillan.

Pires, R. (2008). Regulamentação da participação no OP em Belo Horizonte: eficiência distributiva aliada ao planejamento urbano. In A. Marquetti, G. Campos, & R. Pires (Eds.), *Democracia Participativa e Redistribuição: análise de experiências de orçamento participativo* (pp. 55–76). Xamã.

Ribas Vargas, C. (2007). *Democracia participativa e desenvolvimento humano nos municípios brasileiros: Uma análise a partir de Amartya Sen* (Master's Dissertation). Pontifícia Universidade Católica do Rio Grande do Sul.
Romão, W. (2011). Conselheiros do Orçamento Participativo nas franjas da sociedade política. *Lua Nova: Revista de Cultura e Política, 84*, 219–244.
Ross, M. (2006). Is Democracy Good for the Poor? *American Journal of Political Science, 50*(4), 860–874.
Santos, B. (1998). Participatory Budgeting in Porto Alegre: Toward a Redistributive Democracy. *Politics and Society, 26*, 461–510.
Santos, B. (Ed.). (2005). *Democratizing Democracy: Beyond the Liberal Democratic Canon*. Verso.
Schattschneider, E. E. (1960). *The Semisovereign People: A Realist's View of Democracy in America*. Holt, Rinehart and Winston.
Schneider, A. & Baquero, M. (2006). Get What You Want, Give What You Can: Embedded Public Finance in Porto Alegre. Working Paper 266. Centre for the Future State.
Schugurensky, D. (2006). "This Is Our School of Citizenship": Informal Learning in Local Democracy. *Counterpoints, 249*, 163–182.
Touchton, M., Sugiyama, N. B., & Wampler, B. (2017). Democracy at Work: Moving Beyond Elections to Improve Well-Being. *American Political Science Review, 111*(1), 68–82.
Touchton, M., & Wampler, B. (2014). Improving Social Well-Being Through New Democratic Institutions. *Comparative Political Studies, 47*(10), 1442–1469.
Touchton, M., Wampler, B., & Peixoto, T. (2020). Of Democratic Governance and Revenue: Participatory Institutions and Tax Generation in Brazil. *Governance, 34*, 1193–1212. https://doi.org/10.1111/gove.12552
Wampler, B. (2007). *Participatory Budgeting in Brazil: Contestation, Cooperation, and Accountability*. Pennsylvania State University Press.
Wampler, B. (2015). *Activating Democracy in Brazil: Popular Participation, Social Justice, and Interlocking Institutions*. University of Notre Dame Press.
Wampler, B., & Touchton, M. (2019). Designing Institutions to Improve Social Well-Being: Evidence from Across Brazil's Participatory Budgeting Programs. *European Journal of Political Research, 58*(3), 915–937.
World Bank. (2008). *Brazil: Toward a More Inclusive and Effective Participatory Budget inPorto Alegre (Report No. 40144-BR)*. World Bank.

CHAPTER 6

The Slow Decline of PB from 2005 to 2020

Abstract The spread of participatory budgeting slowed in 2005 as fewer municipalities adopted it for the first time, and it was discontinued by many governments that previously adopted it. The decline accelerated over the next several mayoral terms, with a significant decrease in the numbers as well as program quality by the 2017–2020 period. In this chapter, we show how the changing fortunes of the Workers' Party led it away from promoting PB, how the creation of a broader participatory architecture greatly increased citizen and CSOs participation opportunities (and thus decreased the perceived need for PB), how a generational shift in civil society suggested a move away from institutionalized participation, and how recentralization and, eventually, fiscal crisis reduced mayors' ability to implement PB.

Keywords Participatory budgeting • Workers' Party • Brazil • Participatory institutions • Democracy • Civil Society • Mayors • Decentralization

The spread of participatory budgeting slowed in 2005 as fewer municipalities adopted it for the first time, and it was discontinued by many governments that previously adopted it. The decline accelerated over the next several mayoral terms, with a significant decrease in the numbers as

B. Wampler, B. Goldfrank, *The Rise, Spread, and Decline of Brazil's Participatory Budgeting*,
https://doi.org/10.1007/978-3-030-90058-8_6

well as program quality by the 2017–2020 period. As Fig. 6.1 shows, the spread of PB doesn't match the classic S-shaped curve that is a prominent feature of the diffusion debates, whereby governments continue to adopt a policy innovation until most available units adopt it. Instead, we find an inverted U, suggesting that this innovative democratic institution slowly petered out as fewer and fewer elected governments were interested in adopting it.

To explain why local governments moved away from adopting PB, we again draw from internal, vertical, and horizontal factors shaping the incentive structures mayors faced. In this chapter, we show how the changing fortunes of the Workers' Party led it away from promoting PB, how the creation of a broader participatory architecture greatly increased citizen and CSOs participation opportunities (and thus decreased the perceived need for PB), how a generational shift suggested a move away from institutionalized participation, and how recentralization and, eventually, fiscal crisis reduced mayors' ability to implement PB.

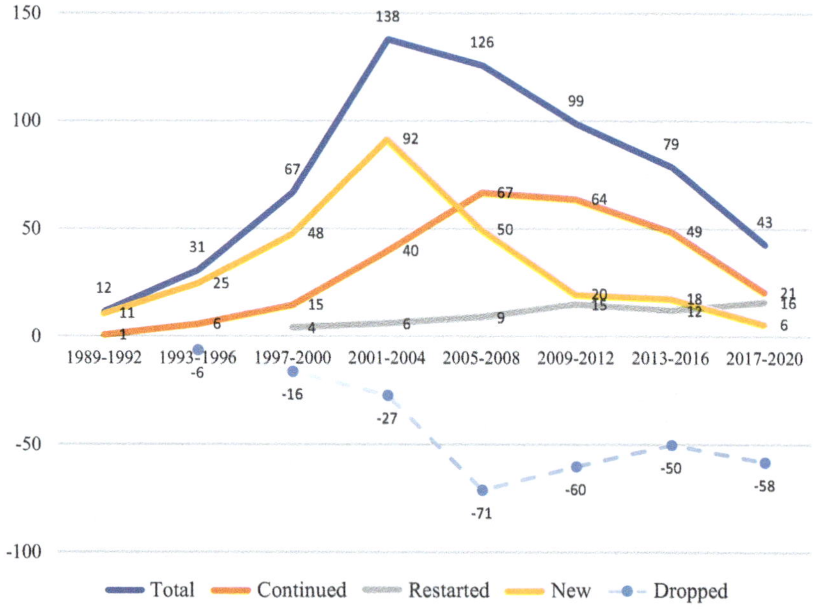

Fig. 6.1 The arc of participatory budgeting

Broadly, we are interested also in knowing if PB's decline is the result of being part of a "policy bubble," which occurs "when governments overinvest in a single policy instrument beyond its instrumental value in achieving a policy goal and that overinvestment is sustained over a relatively long period of time" (Jones et al., 2014, 149). In other words, did governments adopt PB in the absence of clear evidence, which led to an overinvestment? PB received a lot of national and international attention, both among leftists and social progressives as well as among more established international organizations such as the World Bank (Goldfrank, 2012; Peck & Theodore, 2015; Porto de Oliveira, 2017). Ironically, PB began to spread across the world during the post-2004 period, just as it began to decline in use in Brazil (Dias, 2018; Wampler et al., 2021). We first examine the internal factors that led fewer Brazilian municipalities to use PB.

Internal Factors

The political, economic, and social contexts that mayors faced in the 2000s and 2010s were significantly different than the contexts of the late 1980s and 1990s. This changing context helps to explain why fewer and fewer mayors adopted PB programs. At a macro-level, Brazil's democracy was moving strongly and clearly toward consolidation. At the national level, there was regular competition in presidential elections between two parties—the PSDB and the PT. Although local party systems were not as consolidated as those at the national level, they were more consolidated in the mid-2000s than in the late 1980s and early 1990s. Importantly, there was a general consolidation of party brands, which meant that mayors had less to gain by promoting radical innovation. The institutionalization and routinization of democratic practices decreased the needs and political incentives for mayors to experiment with new types of democracy. The proliferation of democratic experiments was crucial to the reformist agenda of mayors in the early to mid-1990s, but it was less important in the 2000s. As developed in Chap. 2 (see Table 2.1), there are four analytical categories that we utilize to best explain governments' incentives to adopt PB: mayoral interest, party competition, civil society, and resources.

Broadly, when we analyze mayoral interests, we need to acknowledge that Workers' Party mayors might have quite different interests than mayors from other parties because PB became associated with the Workers' Party "brand." Workers' Party mayors, who were crucial to the spread of

PB across Brazil during the 1990s and early 2000s, adopted PB at much lower rates beginning in 2005, thus marking a significant turn in how their municipal governments would govern. The Workers' Party increased its electoral victories in cities of over 50,000 inhabitants in every election from 1996 to 2008, but adoption of PB by PT governments began to wane starting in 2005. Table 6.1 shows that the percentage of PT governments using PB decreases with each mayoral administration, from 64% (2005) to 49% (2009) to 33% (2013) to 13% (2017). By the 2017–2020 term, the PT was no more likely to adopt PB than other parties on the left like the PPS, PV, and PSB, who adopted participating budgeting at the rates of 11%, 18%, and 13%, respectively. The incentives for mayors in general to adopt PB declined, but especially for PT mayors. What explains why PT governments withdrew their support for PB? Something shifted in the political environment that led PT governments to adopt PB at much lower rates.

First, the evidence shows that there is no clear association between the Workers' Party using PB and winning elections (see Table 6.2 below); there is no clear evidence that PB would help governments win re-election. Initially, the most prominent PT municipalities with PB were in the large cities of Porto Alegre, Belo Horizonte, and Santo André; these governments won re-election multiple times, helping to create an association between the presence of PB and a successful re-election campaign.[1] For

Table 6.1 Workers' Party and PB

Mayoral term	*Total PB programs*	*Total PT governments*	*Total PT governments with PB*	*PT governments using PB*
1993–1996	31	17	15	88%
1997–2000	67	28	26	93%
2001–2004	138	62	55	89%
2005–2008	126	74	47	64%
2009–2012	99	102	50	49%
2013–2016	79	101	33	33%
2017–2020	43	24	3	13%

[1] We note that the municipality of São Paulo adopted PB during the mayoral term of Luiza Erundina (1989–1992), but that it wasn't a core part of her political or policy agenda. Although the Workers' Party lost the 1992 elections, there is limited evidence and analysis suggesting that her relatively weak PB program was associated with the PT's electoral loss.

Table 6.2 Re-election rates for parties using PB

Election year	*PT government re-elected while using PB*	*PT government re-elected but not using PB*	*PMDB government re-elected while using PB*	*PMDB government re-elected but not using PB*	*PSDB government re-elected while using PB*	*PSDB government re-elected but not using PB*
1996	4 of 15 27%	0 of 2 0%	0 of 4 0%	N/A	2 of 7 29%	N/A
2000	15 of 26 58%	1 of 2 50%	33%	33%	20%	44%
2004	23 of 55 42%	4 of 7 57%	58%	30%	18%	33%
2008	34 of 47 72%	18 of 27 67%	70%	43%	43%	41%
2012	22 of 50 44%	11 of 52 21%	43%	28%	63%	26%
2016	1 of 33 3%	9 of 78 12%	0%	22%	60%	40%

example, in Porto Alegre, the Workers' Party won four consecutive elections, thus creating a connection between investing in vibrant PB processes and winning elections. But the PT lost the 2004 election in Porto Alegre, suggesting that the use of PB was not an electoral silver bullet. In another prominent case, the important city of Belo Horizonte, the Workers' Party was in power across four mayoral terms (1993–2008), but lost the 2008 election. The evidence demonstrates that the adoption of PB by local governments didn't necessarily result in the governing party's re-election.

As described in Chap. 5, there is a body of research that demonstrates that municipalities using PB are associated with improvements in well-being, such as greater spending on health care and sanitation, greater declines in infant mortality rates, and increases in local government tax collection (Gonçalves, 2014; Marquetti, 2003; Marquetti et al., 2008; Touchton et al., 2020; Touchton & Wampler, 2014; Wampler & Touchton, 2019; World Bank, 2008). Given that researchers identified these positive associations taking place in the 2000s, why did this not help governments, especially Workers' Party governments, win re-election? One answer is found in the voting behavior literature. Johannessen (n.d.) argues that although Brazilian voters often claim that they want better health care and education, they are more likely to be motivated by spending on highly visible projects. Johannessen argues:

> citizens use local elections to reward and punish incumbent mayors, but only for actions with highly visible outcomes: Voters reward incumbents for spending on public works projects, capital purchases, and—to a lesser extent—the provision of free goods, but there is no evidence that they reward incumbents for additional spending in their preferred issue areas of health care and education. Notably, these patterns are inconsistent with both voters' stated preferences and their explanations of their decision-making process. (Johannessen, n.d., 3)

In the context of PB's decline, we infer from the existing data that the political payoffs provided by the implementation of relatively small infrastructure projects were not sufficient to mobilize voters beyond the community where the project was implemented. PB programs generally channel community organizations to focus on securing community-level improvements in infrastructure. These public works projects are highly visible to the specific community that secures the specific project, but they aren't always visible to the broader city. For example, in Belo Horizonte, the PB program brought sewage lines to a hilly *favela*, which had a major impact on neighborhood residents' quality of life (Wampler, 2007, 2015). Although this project benefited tens of thousands of local residents, it wasn't readily visible to Belo Horizonte's 2.2 million other residents. Thus, a key explanation for why PB doesn't have major re-election outcomes is that the implementation of relatively small-scale projects may not be sufficiently strong to influence citywide electoral disputes.

A second compelling explanation for why PT municipal governments distanced themselves from PB is provided by Santos et al. (2020), who examine the role of the PT's infamous internal divisions; the party was able to minimize splits and desertions and achieve relative cohesion for a diverse body of leftists only by allowing distinct internal political factions to persist. As has been well-documented, Lula and his allies created the largest group, the "Majority Camp," in the mid-1990s following the PT's disastrous showing in the 1994 presidential elections (Samuels, 2004). Santos and his co-authors (2020) use the election results from internal PT elections to show that the greater the vote share for the dominant political group within the PT, the Majority Camp, the less likely the municipality was to adopt PB in the 2005–2012 period. In other words, the greater the presence of leftist political factions within the Workers' Party at the municipal level, the more likely that the PT would adopt PB if and when the party won the municipal election. As Table 6.1, above, demonstrates, the adoption rate by PT governments began to drop dramatically even while the PT saw its fortunes improve at the polls in Brazil's larger cities.

The city of São Paulo illuminates this process. The Workers' Party elected Marta Suplicy to office of the mayor in 2000. Suplicy had limited connections to the Workers' Party social movement base and she wasn't strongly committed to participatory democracy. Within her government, the most radical faction of the Workers' Party, known as the Democratic Socialists, strongly promoted PB and the deepening of the democracy as the means to connect with poor citizens. The Democratic Socialists were a relatively small faction within Sao Paulo's PT as well as across Brazil, thus suggesting that PB was being driven by a relatively small group with the PT (Wampler, 2007, Chapter 6).

Moving beyond parties, another important reason for the decline was a shift in the configuration of civil society activism, mobilization, and organization during the 2000s. The 1980s and early 1990s were marked by extensive civil society mobilization around issues of access to health care, education, basic infrastructure, the environment, and housing (Alvarez, 1990; Dagnino, 1994, 1998). By 2005, civil society mobilization was more diffuse, institutionalized, and policy-oriented. Mass mobilizations, especially by the political left, declined, as the political moment shifted from the transition and creation of democracy to the institutionalization of participation within government-led venues, and most prominently, in public policy councils that engaged NGO and social movement leaders rather than mobilizing the broader citizenry. In addition, the demobilization was driven by a booming economy in the 2000s, which led many young individuals to seek out jobs and employment, as well as by the sense that Brazil had returned to "normal" politics after 15+ years of stable democratic elections. The Workers' Party, as discussed in Chaps. 1 and 3, was founded by social movements, union members, and parts of the progressive middle class; the demobilization of social movements and the shrinking size of unions meant that the Workers' Party could no longer count on social movements to turn out large numbers of voters as well as PB participants; the demobilization of Brazil's civil society decreases the political incentives for all mayors, but especially Workers' Party mayors, to adopt PB.

Finally, the Fiscal Responsibility Law (*Lei de Responsabilidade Fiscal*) re-centralized many resources, thus hampering mayors' fiscal flexibility (Bezerra, 2016). This is also a vertical factor, but we include it here because the level of resources directly affects internal motivations to adopt PB. As we argued in Chap. 3, the decentralization of resources during the 1990s generated a significant level of additional municipal revenues that many mayors were able to allocate toward PB programs. Because these were "new" funds, resulting from the fiscal decentralization, special interest groups, unions, and so on didn't necessarily control access to these funds. By the mid-2000s, recentralization after 15+ years of decentralization narrowed mayors' fiscal flexibility, thus making PB less attractive. Moreover, Brazil's downward economic spiral in the 2010s led to a fiscal crisis; as municipal governments' tax revenues shrank, the funding available for PB diminished as well, a problem which only worsened under austerity policies of the latter half of the 2010s (Fedozzi et al., 2018, 118–119). Quantitative analysis by Bezerra and Junqueira (2018) finds that, even after controlling for partisanship of the mayor, cities with smaller per capita budgets are less likely to adopt PB, while cities with a lower investment rate are less likely to continue PB.

Simply put, mayors in cities with PB found themselves unable to keep up with citizen demands over time. In Recife, which used PB from 1993 to 2012, the municipal administration built up a backlog of over 1000 projects that had been approved through PB but never implemented (Azevedo, 2019, 62). The inability to complete approved projects affected even the flagship cases of PB in Porto Alegre and Belo Horizonte. In the 1990s, Workers' Party administrations in both cities were able to complete nearly 100% of the projects approved through PB. In the 2005–2010 period, the municipal administration in Porto Alegre concluded only 47% of approved projects (Melgar, 2015, 39), and the value of the projects completed declined precipitously as well, from about 524 million *reais* in the 2001–2004 period to only 18 million *reais* in the 2013–2016 period (Siqueira & Marzulo, 2020, 414). According to Azevedo (2019, 62), by 2017 the backlog reached 2400 projects in Porto Alegre and the mayor suspended that year's PB assemblies. In Belo Horizonte, the administration switched PB from an annual to a biennial process in 1999 to reduce the number of projects each year; even then, a backlog of some 700 projects was evident by 2014 (Montambeault, 2019, 40). In the face of government incapacity to carry out projects, PB loses credibility among city residents, as reflected in declining numbers of participants. Mayors, in turn, go from viewing PB as a welcome way of demonstrating their transparency and accountability to seeing PB as a liability that can clearly show their failure to keep their promises. The difficulty of reliably executing the projects prioritized by their constituents helps explain why a growing number of mayors decided not to re-adopt PB in the 2000s and 2010s, as seen in Fig. 6.1.

Horizontal

PB spread across Brazil during the 1993–2004 period through horizontal connections. Municipal governments learned from each other and participated in policy networks where they learned about PB and related policy innovations. In the post-2004 period, the horizontal connections among governments gradually changed focus away from PB or simply weakened, thus helping to explain why fewer governments were willing to adopt. The Instituto Cajamar, for example, had already closed its doors in 1996; FASE reduced the number of cities in which it operated; and while the FNPP never officially ended, its work gradually dried up. There are several compelling reasons for why these horizontal connections withered.

First, the spoiling of the PT's "good government" brand helps to account for why some "PB-curious" governments would be more reluctant to adopt PB (Goldfrank & Wampler, 2008, 2017). In 2002, Celso Daniel, the two-time mayor of Santo André and Lula's presidential campaign manager, was murdered under mysterious circumstances (Fausto, 2005). Daniel had been an early champion of PB, adopting it during his two terms in office. However, following his murder, accusations of corruption in Santo André led to claims that suggest that the PT's self-promotion as a "clean, transparent party" wasn't all true. Rather, the party relied on dirty money and creative accounting practices like all other parties in Brazil. In 2005, President Lula's administration was embroiled by the *mensalão* (monthly payment) scandal, accused of paying bribes to legislators in exchange for their support. The scandal severely tarnished the PT's reputation for "good government" and for doing things differently. Part of the PT's defense of its actions was that it was merely building on a political strategy created by its predecessors, the PSDB, but for many Brazilians, that was the problem—the PT billed itself as being different but resorted to using the same underhanded strategies as all the other parties. From a "horizontal diffusion" perspective, the spoiling of the PT's good government brand meant that municipal governments were less willing to adopt PB because the positive association with the PB was tarnished by the PT's actions in other areas.

Second, political competition and coalition-building changed during the 2000s. Competition decreases the incentives for local governments to adopt policy programs associated with their rivals. As Table 6.3 demonstrates, most newly elected governments always chose not to continue PB, except for the 2001–2004 period. One possible explanation for this exception is that the PT's Lula was the clear favorite in the 2002 presidential race, and several parties wished to show that they were good potential allies in the ensuing government.

This ties directly into another important phenomenon: an "anti-PT" (*antipetismo*) attitude strengthened across civil society and among voters under President Dilma Rousseff, aided by the traditional news media as well as new social media (Davis & Straubhaar, 2020; Samuels & Zucco, 2018). The massive protests in 2013 and 2014 were initially led by leftist political activists seeking to improve the quality of public transportation and to lower its cost. The protests led to a broader mobilization that came to be dominated by conservative groups (Saad-Filho, 2013). During the protests, there wasn't a strong call for the expansion of participatory institutions, as there had been in the 1980s and 1990s (Abers & Tatagiba, 2016; Pogrebinschi & Tanscheit, 2017). Rather, movement leaders drew attention to issues of public corruption, administrative mismanagement, and an economic slowdown, which helped to spread an "anti-PT" attitude throughout the country. These public protests helped set up the conditions that led to the eventual impeachment and removal from office of President Dilma Rousseff in 2016. The strengthening of this anti-PT current in the mid-2010s helps explain the sharp dip in PB adoption in the last municipal term analyzed, 2017–2020.

Table 6.3 Continuing to use PB after government changes hands

Mayoral term	*When governments change hands, what % of newly elected governments continue to use PB?*	*When the PT loses, what % of newly elected governments continue to use PB?*
1993–1996	33%	20%
1997–2000	40%	18%
2001–2004	60%	23%
2005–2008	37%	32%
2009–2012	26%	32%
2013–2016	32%	33%
2017–2020	25%	15%

Third, the FGV "innovations in Good Governance" programs were slowly wound down during the 2004–2008 period. The Ford Foundation started the international leg of the program in the late 1990s in Brazil, South Africa, India, the Philippines, and Chile. Importantly, this meant that the FGV good governance network had a more limited reach—it wasn't able to connect with municipal governments in the ways that it had previously done. In the absence of a public policy institute providing guidance about PB's potential benefits and shortcomings, PB wasn't as prominently featured in good governance networks within Brazil, even as the World Bank, USAID, the UNDP, and other international organizations began promoting PB on a global scale (Porto de Oliveira, 2017).

Vertical

There are three vertical factors that help explain the decline in PB. First, after the PT won Brazil's greatest political prize in 2002, with Lula's election to the presidency, the Workers' Party turned its attention away from PB. The PT's 2002 election platform included a reference to adopting PB at the federal level, but little came of this electoral pledge. As noted in Table 6.1, above, the rate of PT municipal governments adopting PB *declined* during Lula's two terms as President. Instead of promoting PB, the PT invested its resources into promoting participation in national public policy conferences (Pogrebinschi & Samuels, 2014; Pogrebinschi & Santos, 2011). Under President Lula (2003–2006; 2007–2010) and President Dilma (2011–2014; 2015–2016), the federal government held 81 national conferences that incorporated between 6 and 9 million individual participants (although many were likely the same individuals who participated in multiple venues) (Pogrebinschi & Samuels, 2014; Pogrebinschi & Santos, 2011). The policy conferences relied on mass mobilization and were vertically integrated (municipal, state, federal). PB-type venues also rely on mass mobilization but focus on local communities and municipal politics.

Under President Lula, PB became an "orphan" at the national level because there wasn't a core member of the PT national government who advocated using PB at the national level or promoting PB at the municipal level (Daniel Avelino. Interview. April 22, 2020). Rather, the PT's political interest in connecting mass mobilization to policy and legislation came through the conferences. As Pogrebinschi and Samuels (2014) demonstrate, holding a national conference was associated with subsequent executive orders and legislation that reflected the general priorities of the conferences. For the national government, the conferences were attractive because they were non-binding, allowing policy and political signals to be sent between the "base" and the national government, and because they involved the mass mobilization of millions into government-sanctioned participatory venues.

Second, the proliferation of municipal public policy councils provided additional opportunities for citizen participation without the need for PB. After PB was founded in the late 1980s, there were three main models of institutionalized participation: public policy management councils in specific arenas (e.g., health, education), conferences in specific policy arenas, and PB. The councils were more institutionalized, drew on smaller numbers of participants, and included extensive government representation (Avritzer, 2009; Wampler et al., 2020). Over the course of the 1990s and early 2000s, the federal government began mandating the use of policy councils in five policy arenas (education, health, social service, child protection services, and children and adolescents). By 2005, over 95% of all municipalities had these councils, with the smallest municipalities (under 10,000 residents) accounting for the majority of the cities lacking councils (Santos Barreto, 2011; Wampler, 2015; Wampler et al., 2020). There was nearly 100% coverage in municipalities with more than 50,000 residents, which is the sample size for this project.

By 2011, there were an estimated 60,000 municipal-level councils across Brazil (Pires, 2011; Santos Barreto, 2011; Wampler, 2015). These councils have a minimum of 5 citizen representatives, which means that at least 300,000 citizens had a seat on councils that had policymaking and budgetary authority. The presence of councils decreased CSO activists' demand for PB because they came to have multiple parallel policy venues in which to work on policy-related issues. The proliferation of these councils coincided with an increasing professionalization of CSOs and NGOs during the 2000s and 2010s (Alvarez, 1999). Councils at the municipal level are institutionalized, which enables them to remain in place even in the face of a disinterested or hostile executive. There is, of course, wide variation in how many of these councils function, but the relevant issue is that CSO activists chose (or were channeled) into working within these councils, thus diminishing the need for PB. Likewise, because the councils were mandated from above, municipal governments spent their scarce time and energy on implementing and activating the council system (in addition to the time spent organizing the municipal-level conferences), which diminished their interest and ability in maintaining or building new PB programs.[2]

Third, Brazil's funding structure is based on a system in which the federal government collects revenues and then transfers resources to states and municipal governments. Municipal governments typically collect between 2 and 5% of their overall budgets from local sources (such as property and sales taxes or user fees). Following the promulgation of the 1988 Constitution, municipal governments gained access to greater resources and they also had more service delivery responsibilities (Montero & Samuels, 2004; Wampler et al., 2020). But the federal government began to recentralize resources at the end of the 1990s, which ended the ten-year period of greater municipal-level financial flexibility (Spada, 2014). The federal government, in order to limit local corruption and the use of public monies for election campaigns, created greater restrictions on how municipalities could spend their resources. For example, municipalities were required to spend 30% on education and 25% on health services as well as no more than 50% on personnel. Although these federal rules were designed to promote "good governance" (transparency, accountability, etc.), one unintended consequence is that they diminish local governments' ability to innovate. Because local budgets were more constrained, local governments were less likely to dedicate more political and policy space to citizen engagement in the budget (Bezerra & Junqueira, 2018).

In sum, the broad expansion of participatory institutions greatly increased opportunities for citizens and governments to engage combined with the simultaneous recentralization of resources and tightening of budget rules to decrease the political payoffs for governments to adopt PB while simultaneously drawing community activists into participatory institutions other than PB. The decline of PB across Brazil is thus directly associated with the building of other participatory institutions.

[2] The less intensive nature of the public policy conferences (because they are infrequent and short-lived) and the policy councils (because they do not involve mass mobilization) help explain why some scholars of Brazilian cities view the Lula era as one of "abandonment of participatory processes" (Lara, 2014, 259).

Conclusion

Brazil's shifting political landscape across the 2000s led to a decline in the adoption of PB. The institutional and political incentives changed, thus decreasing elected governments' interest in adopting PB. Most importantly, the Workers' Party offered much more limited support for PB than it had provided in the 1990s. After all, in the 1990s, the Workers' Party was a relatively small opposition political party that sought to build a new political project by inverting the local policy priorities and recrafting the means through which people engage the state. In 2003, President Lula took office, giving the Workers' Party control of one of the world's largest governments. Following Lula's victory, the Workers' Party won municipal elections at higher rates than ever in 2004, 2008, and 2012, but their governments grew increasingly less likely to adopt PB. In 2016, the Workers' Party had its worst showing since 1992, winning just 24 larger municipalities. Almost all chose not to adopt PB, thus ending a 30-year period in which the majority of PB programs in Brazil were in municipalities controlled by the Workers' Party. By the 2017–2020 period, both the Workers' Party and PB played a limited role in urban politics in Brazil.

Broadly, Brazilian mayors' use of PB—a flurry of adoption in many of Brazil's largest cities in the 1990s and early 2000s, followed by fewer and fewer new adoptions and eventual discontinuation of existing programs—fits Jones et al.'s description of a policy bubble. There was considerable excitement around PB in the 1990s and early 2000s, but most of the excitement had waned in Brazil by the mid-2000s. Although empirical evidence would show that PB was positively associated with social and political change, elected governments overestimated PB's impact on voters as well as its potential for radical transformation. In the end, PB generates positive, but incremental, change that can help generate meaningful improvements in the quality of people's lives. However, PB alone does not produce radical change that reorganizes local political life. PB's decline can thus be viewed as a policy bubble whereby many governments and civil society allies were enthralled by its transformational potential but moved away from the program when it became increasingly apparent that PB would produce a relatively small amount of change. The decline of PB came as governments began investing their time and effort into other participatory and policy projects.

References

Abers, R., & Tatagiba, L. (2016). Institutional Activism: Mobilizing for Women's Health from Inside the Brazilian Bureaucracy. In F. Rossi & M. Von Bülow (Eds.), *Social Movement Dynamics* (pp. 72–101). Routledge.

Alvarez, S. (1990). *Engendering Democracy in Brazil: Women in Transition Politics*. Princeton University Press.

Alvarez, S. (1999). Advocating Feminism: The Latin American Feminist NGO 'Boom'. *International Feminist Journal of Politics, 1*(2), 181–209.

Avritzer, L. (2009). *Participatory Institutions in Democratic Brazil*. Woodrow Wilson Center.

Azevedo, U. (2019). *Análise do declínio do número de implementações e do aumento do abandono das experiências de Orçamento Participativo no Brasil (2004-2016)* (Master's Thesis). UNICAMP.

Bezerra, C. (2016). *Por que o Orçamento Participativo entrou em declínio no Brasil. Mudanças na legislação fiscal e seu impacto sobre a estratégia partidária*. VII Seminário Discente da Pós-Graduação em Ciência Política da USP.

Bezerra, C., & Junqueira, M. (2018). *Why Has Participatory Budgeting Adoption Declined in Brazil?* 114th Annual Meeting of the American Political Science Association, Boston, Massachusetts.

Dagnino, E. (1994). *Os Anos 90: Politica e Sociedade no Brasil*. Editora Brasiliense.

Dagnino, E. (1998). The Cultural Politics of Citizenship, Democracy and the State. In S. Alvarez, S. E. Dagnino, & A. Escobar (Eds.), *Cultures of Politics/ Politics of Cultures: Re-visioning Latin American Social Movements*. Westview Press.

Davis, S., & Straubhaar, J. (2020). Producing Antipetismo: Media Activism and the Rise of the Radical, Nationalist Right in Contemporary Brazil. *International Communication Gazette, 82*(1), 82–100.

Dias, N. (Ed.). (2018). *Hope for Democracy: 30 Years of Participatory Budgeting Worldwide*. Oficina.

Fausto, R. (2005). Para além da gangrene. *Lua Nova, 65*, 203–228.

Fedozzi, L., Furtado, A., & Rangel, R. (2018). Participatory Budgeting in Brazil: Elements for a Brief Evaluation. In N. Días (Ed.), *Hope for Democracy: 30 Years of Participatory Budgeting Worldwide*. Oficina.

Goldfrank, B. (2012). The World Bank and the Globalization of Participatory Budgeting. *Journal of Public Deliberation, 8*(2), 7.

Goldfrank, B., & Wampler, B. (2008). From the Petista Way of Governing to the Brazilian Way: How the PT Changed. *Revista Debates, 2*(2), 245–271.

Goldfrank, B., & Wampler, B. (2017). Good Government and Politics as Usual: The Schizophrenic Path of the Workers' Party. In P. Kingstone & T. Power (Eds.), *Democratic Brazil Divided*. University of Pittsburgh.

Gonçalves, S. (2014). The Effects of Participatory Budgeting on Municipal Expenditures and Infant Mortality in Brazil. *World Development, 53*, 94–110.
Johannessen, P. (n.d.). *Visibility and Local Electoral Accountability*. Unpublished Working Paper.
Jones, B., Thomas, H., III, & Wolfe, M. (2014). Policy Bubbles. *Policy Studies Journal, 42*(1), 146–171.
Lara, F. L. (2014). Cidades na era Lula o lento abandono dos processos participativos. *Revista do Instituto de Estudos Brasileiros, 58*, 245–262.
Marquetti, A. (2003). Democracia, Equidade e Effciencia, o Caso do Orçamento Participativo em Porto Alegre. In L. Avritzer & Z. Navarro (Eds.), *A Inovação Democrática no Brasil: O Orçamento Participativo* (pp. 129–156). Cortez Editores.
Marquetti, A., Campos, G., & Pires, R. (2008). *Democracia participativa e redistribuição: análise de experiências de orçamento participativo*. Xamã.
Melgar, T. (2015). The Perilous Paths of Deeper Democracy: Understanding the Rise and Decline of Participatory Budgeting in Porto Alegre, Brazil. *Social Science Diliman, 11*(2), 24–55.
Montambeault, F. (2019). It Was Once a Radical Democratic Proposal: Theories of Gradual Institutional Change in Brazilian Participatory Budgeting. *Latin American Politics and Society, 61*(1), 29–53.
Montero, A. P., & Samuels, D. J. (2004). *Decentralization and Democracy in Latin America*. University of Notre Dame Press.
Peck, J., & Theodore, N. (2015). *Fast Policy: Experimental Statecraft at the Thresholds of Neoliberalism*. University of Minnesota Press.
Pires, R. (2011). *Efetividade das instituições participativas no Brasil: estratégias de avaliação*. IPEA.
Pogrebinschi, T., & Samuels, D. (2014). The Impact of Participatory Democracy: Evidence from Brazil's National Public Policy Conferences. *Comparative Politics, 46*(3), 313–332.
Pogrebinschi, T., & Santos, F. (2011). Participação como representação: o impacto das conferências nacionais de políticas públicas no Congresso Nacional. *Dados, 54*(3), 259–305.
Pogrebinschi, T., & Tanscheit, T. (2017). *Moving Backwards–What Happened to Citizen Participation in Brazil?* Retrieved August 1, 2021, from www.latinno.wzb.eu
Porto de Oliveira, O. (2017). *International Policy Diffusion and Participatory Budgeting: Ambassadors of Participation, International Institutions and Transnational Networks*. Palgrave Macmillan.
Saad-Filho, A. (2013). Mass Protests Under 'Left Neoliberalism': Brazil, June-July 2013. *Critical Sociology, 39*(5), 657–669.

Samuels, David. 2004. From Socialism to Social Democracy: Party Organization and the Transformation of the Workers' Party in Brazil. *Comparative Political Studies, 37*, 999–1024.
Samuels, D., & Zucco, C. (2018). *Partisans, Antipartisans, and Nonpartisans: Voting Behavior in Brazil.* Cambridge University Press.
Santos Barreto, D. (2011). Pesquisa de Informacoes Basicas. In R. Pires (Ed.), *Efetividade das Instituições Participativas no Brasil: Estratégias de Avaliação.* IPEA.
Santos, F., Tanscheit, T., & Ventura, T. (2020). O Partido dos Trabalhadores e as instituições Participativas: a influência da dinâmica intrapartidária na adoção do Orçamento Participativo. *Dados, 63*(3), 1–37.
Siqueira, L. F., & Marzulo, E. P. (2020). Da democracia participativa à desdemocratização na cidade: a experiência do Orçamento Participativo em Porto Alegre. *Cadernos Metrópole, 23*, 399–422.
Spada, P. (2014). *The Diffusion of Participatory Governance Innovations: A Panel Data Analysis of the Adoption and Survival of Participatory Budgeting in Brazil.* Annual Conference of the Latin American Studies Association.
Touchton, M., & Wampler, B. (2014). Improving Social Well-Being Through New Democratic Institutions. *Comparative Political Studies, 47*(10), 1442–1469.
Touchton, M., Wampler, B., & Peixoto, T. (2020). Of Democratic Governance and Revenue: Participatory Institutions and Tax Generation in Brazil. *Governance, 34*, 1193–1212. https://doi.org/10.1111/gove.12552
Wampler, B. (2007). *Participatory Budgeting in Brazil: Contestation, Cooperation, and Accountability.* Pennsylvania State University Press.
Wampler, B. (2015). *Activating Democracy in Brazil: Popular Participation, Social Justice, and Interlocking Institutions.* University of Notre Dame Press.
Wampler, B., McNulty, S., & Touchton, M. (2021). *Participatory Budgeting in Global Perspective.* Oxford University Press.
Wampler, B., Sugiyama, N., & Touchton, M. (2020). *Democracy at Work: Pathways to Well-Being in Brazil.* Cambridge University Press.
Wampler, B., & Touchton, M. (2019). Designing Institutions to Improve Social Well-Being: Evidence from Across Brazil's Participatory Budgeting Programs. *European Journal of Political Research, 58*(3), 915–937.
World Bank. (2008). *Brazil: Toward a More Inclusive and Effective Participatory Budget in Porto Alegre (Report No. 40144-BR).* World Bank.

CHAPTER 7

Conclusion

Abstract This conclusion has three main sections. First, we highlight what PB's arc in Brazil tells us about democratic innovations, the role of parties and party systems vis-à-vis participatory institutions, civil society, state capacity, and the quality of democracy. In the second section, we look at what Brazil's PB arc can help us learn about other cases across the globe. We expect that PB will continue to spread across the globe, but our analysis suggests that many cities adopting PB are likely to either move to more restricted forms (e.g., those in the Philippines and Uruguay), simply abandon it (Kerala, India; Durban, South Africa), or a combination of each (those in Chile and Spain). In the third and final section, we turn to the question: Where does PB go from here? Our analysis is rooted in both pessimistic and optimistic viewpoints; we have a number of concerns that suggest that the spread of PB will not produce the positive results that were identified in Brazil. But we also see hopeful signs in some places that PB can act in a way that promotes its founding ideals.

Keywords Global spread of participatory budgeting • Future of participatory budgeting

B. Wampler, B. Goldfrank, *The Rise, Spread, and Decline of Brazil's Participatory Budgeting*,
https://doi.org/10.1007/978-3-030-90058-8_7

Participatory budgeting is a democratic institution that establishes a delicate balance between deliberation, mass mobilization, equity considerations, and incremental policymaking. The creation, spread, and decline of PB programs offer an important window for understanding the evolution of Brazilian democracy between 1990 and 2020. PB programs are inserted within the broader logic of representative democracy; in the Brazilian context, these programs represent an effort to move beyond the confines of actual existing democracy to "deepen" the quality of democracy (Avritzer, 2002; Fung & Wright, 2003; Santos, 2005). A broad body of evidence suggests that PB programs are associated with shifts in public deliberation (Avritzer, 2002; Faria, 2003), civil society organization (Abers, 2000; Baiocchi, 2005; Baiocchi et al., 2011), democratic practices (Goldfrank, 2011; Wampler, 2007), and well-being (Gonçalves, 2014; Touchton & Wampler, 2014; Wampler & Touchton, 2019). Considering that the vast bulk of research on Brazilian PB has considered it successful from policy and democratic standpoints, why wasn't this enough to sustain PB's continued expansion? What can we learn from PB's 30-year arc in Brazil to better understand PB's fate across the rest of the globe? As PB spreads across the globe, will it also fall into a decline as it did in Brazil? Or will PB's new champions continue to sustain it?

The subnational research approach we employed in this book, based on three independent but interactive fields—internal, horizontal, and vertical—provides excellent analytical leverage to explain the creation, spread, and decline of participatory budgeting. Table 7.1, below, illustrates the key factors that led to PB's broader arc. As seen in both Table 7.1 and Fig. 1.1 in the introduction, the Workers' Party (PT) was essential to all phases of PB's arc, partly due to the PT's unique combination of strong ties to social movements and programmatic cohesion.

This conclusion has three main sections. First, we seek to understand what PB's arc in Brazil tells us about democratic innovations, the role of parties and party systems vis-à-vis participatory institutions, civil society, state capacity, and the quality of democracy. This section focuses on Brazil. In the second section, we look at what Brazil's PB arc can help us learn about other cases across the globe. We expect that PB will continue to spread across the globe (in the upward slope of the S-shaped curve as of 2021), but our analysis suggests that many cities adopting PB are likely to either move to more restricted forms (e.g., those in the Philippines and Uruguay), simply abandon it (Kerala, India; Durban, South Africa), or a combination of each (those in Chile and Spain) (see Baiocchi & Ganuza,

Table 7.1 Explaining PB's creation, spread, and decline: overview of 3 periods and 3 levels of analysis

	Creation	*Spread*	*Decline*
Internal	PT wins elections PT experiments with participatory institutions Civil society mobilized and demand increased participation opportunities Decentralization affords more resources, especially to larger cities	PT wins more elections PT aligns with other leftist governments, which also adopt PB PMDB and PSDB governments adopt PB in larger cities Leftist NGOs and CSOs are likely to advocate for PB	Mayors' interest in PB wanes Centrist groups within PT are less likely to support PB; PT slowly winds down support NGOs and CSOs are less likely to advocate for PB Recentralization restricts budgetary autonomy
Horizontal	NGOs, social movements, and PT spread ideas associated with popular participation and PB	National Forum for Popular Participation (FNPP) creates a broad network to promote popular participation Getúlio Vargas Foundation (FGV) promotes innovations and good governance	PT's involvement in corruption scandals makes centrist parties less interested in adopting PB National NGOs and policy networks focus on federal government for programmatic change
Vertical	PT national leadership promotes PB Municipal governments have greater access to revenues due to federal transfers	"PT way of governing" means that almost all PB governments adopt International organizations promote PB within Brazil	Fiscal recentralization and fiscal crisis make PB less appealing National PT no longer actively promotes PB

2017; Goldfrank, 2017; Wampler et al., 2021). In the third and final section, we turn to the question: Where does PB go from here? Our analysis is rooted in both pessimistic and optimistic viewpoints; we have a number of concerns that suggest that the spread of PB will not produce the positive results that were identified in Brazil (see Chap. 5). But we also see hopeful signs in some places that PB can act in a way that promotes its founding ideals.

PB's Arc in Brazil

Broadly, what does PB's 30-year arc tell us about Brazilian politics, society, and democracy? In this section, we seek to move beyond the specificities of PB and place it in the broader context of Brazil.

Democratic Innovations

PB is an innovative democratic institution; its roots lie in both democratic ideals and technical policymaking. PB combines deliberation, mass mobilization, equity considerations, and incremental policymaking (Avritzer, 2002; Baiocchi & Ganuza, 2017; Fedozzi, 1997; Marquetti, 2003). It is the combination of these four factors that make it innovative. Although we see some of these factors in other types of participatory programs, what really makes PB unique is its potential to successfully combine them. When PB programs work well, they can produce a wide range of positive outcomes, from inclusion, voice, and vote for the traditionally excluded to the provision of public goods in poor communities.

During PB's early years, the rules and processes were created through a trial and error process, driven by ideology, political interests, and resources. We think that it is crucial to recognize the PB wasn't "born" whole or complete, but created through experimentation. What didn't work was abandoned; what worked well was strengthened (Fedozzi, 1997). We believe this experimentation in places like Porto Alegre and Belo Horizonte were critical to the development of an institutional design that provided space for mobilization, deliberation, incremental policymaking, and oversight. During the early 1990s, PB's rules and processes consolidated and became recognizable as a distinct institution.

However, we find that innovations within local PB processes tend to decline over time for a number of reasons. First, they decline because once governments and allies find the right set of rules, which balance mass mobilization, deliberation, and policy implementation, the initial need to innovate is removed; there's no need to continue to innovate if things are working. Second, governments and CSOs that benefit from the consolidated set of rules are likely to maintain the existing rules if the rules are working relatively well for them. Third, the Brazilian federal government imposed restrictions on how municipalities could allocate resources, which limited the ability of municipal governments to use resources in new and different ways.

Overall, what is really striking about this period is that PB's arc is quite similar to the arc of democratic innovation in Brazil (Avritzer, 2002). PB was created at the end of a 20-year military dictatorship; during the founding period of the late 1980s and early 1990s, CSOs, social movements, and political parties were interested in experimenting with local democratic institutions. There was a proliferation of policy council adoptions and national conferences became more widely used. By the mid-2000s, the excitement and interest in municipal-level participatory institutions had waned, as many of these democratic institutions were routinized and bureaucratized. By the mid-2010s, Brazil's democracy entered into a crisis, with substantial worry that it was backsliding on basic citizenship rights (Avritzer, 2019).

Parties and Party System

Over the course of PB's 30-year arc covered in this book, Brazil's fragmented party system—with between 20 and 30 parties represented in the Congress—consolidated around four major parties. The leftist PT (winning presidential elections in 2002, 2006, 2010, 2014), the center-right PSDB (winning presidential elections in 1994 and 1998), the catch-all centrist PMDB (electing the vice president in 1985, 1988, 2010, all of whom would become president; holding the largest number of mayors elected from 1988 to 2020), and the conservative PFL/DEM (electing vice president in 1994 and 1998). Among these parties, the Workers' Party was the only one that aligned itself with the emergent civil society and sought to brand itself as "participatory, transparent and inclusive." This political position also bled into an ethical position as many PT officials sought to occupy a moral high ground in which their party was led by honest, working-class individuals who really had the best interests of Brazil at the forefront of their agenda. Why did the Workers' Party, the main force behind the spread of PB, begin to move away from PB? And what does this say about the future of the PT and popular participation?

First, PB programs' electoral dividends were, at best, unclear. In multiple cities, the Workers' Party placed PB at the center of their governing strategy and won consecutive elections (Porto Alegre and Belo Horizonte are two great examples). Yet in other cities governed by the Workers' Party that used PB, the party lost. The ambiguity surrounding PB and electoral results led PT governments to seek other strategies that might help them to win elections. Public investments in more visible projects, such as the

Family Grant Program, the Family Healthcare Program, and large housing and electric projects, were part of the shift under President Lula and can be also be identified under Lula's co-partisan, Fernando Haddad, as mayor of São Paulo in the mid-2010s (Heller, 2019; Hunter, 2010; Samuels & Zucco, 2018).

Second, the centrist, majority faction associated with Lula (the PT's clear, dominant leader), wasn't necessarily a strong supporter of PB. Rather, PB was "carried" by minority factions within the party. The majority faction sought to build wider coalitions among the population to more easily win elections; they didn't view PB as a policy program that would provide the necessary electoral dividends. Following this logic, when the PT won Brazil's presidency, the party didn't invest in PB. Instead, it sought to institutionalize new public policy management councils at the federal level, invested heavily in public policy conferences, and sought to strengthen the new ombudsmen and oversight agency (CGU). President Lula did create an "economic and social development" policy board at the federal level to incorporate "civil society," but it was comprised mostly of well-positioned social, political, and economic elites. President Lula's government made little effort to create a budget-focused participatory process, and President Dilma even less. President Dilma did issue a presidential decree (#8243) in 2014 that sought to initiate a "National System of Social Participation" to promote participation and to improve how the state managed the unwieldy body of participatory institutions, yet the Congress refused to endorse it. Dilma's administration sought to encourage federal departments to more actively use participatory mechanisms and to better coordinate across siloed agencies. However, Dilma's decree was interpreted by her political opponents as an attack on the principles of the 1988 Constitution and as an effort to import ideas and practices from Hugo Chavez's reform project in Venezuela. After acrimonious debate, the decree was never implemented.

In sum, the distancing of the PT from popular participation programs like PB indicates that the party was attempting to find alternative ways of connecting with their followers and potential supporters. The PT no longer strongly advocated for the broader adoption of municipal-level participatory programs as the means through which Brazilian society could be transformed. Given the importance of the Workers' Party in the creation and spread of PB, the party's current ambivalence suggests that PB—or a similar mass mobilization institution—is unlikely to return. PB was part of a broader suite of reforms that ensured traditionally excluded voices would be able to exercise voice and vote in the political system as a key part of the *modo petista de governar*. We would expect that some remnants of this PT way of governing would resurface in the future, as PT mayors search for alternative ways to strengthen their connections to the broader community. However, the PT performed poorly in mayoral races in 2016 and even worse in 2020; it is currently distant from running the municipal governments where new opportunities for policy experimentation might arise.

State Capacity

The larger Brazilian municipalities had reasonably strong state capacity during the late 1980s and early 1990s when PB was being established. Further, they gained access to new revenues (mainly transfers from the federal government, but also property and sales taxes), which strengthened their ability to implement projects selected through PB. As we analyze PB's arc in Brazil, we note the presence of what we are calling the "state capacity trap," which we think helps illuminate why PB is initially quite successful but then encounters barriers that often lead government officials to withdraw their support.

Analytically, the "state capacity trap" works as follows: subnational governments have sufficient capacity to implement small- and medium-sized projects. On the small size, this would include projects like street paving and lighting, small drainage systems, and reforms of schools and health care clinics. Medium-size projects might include building schools and health care clinics, connecting shantytowns to existing sewage and water lines, and building small housing projects (e.g., apartment buildings that are three floors). In Brazil, PB's creation and spread took place in municipalities in which local governments could implement these types of projects; governments were thus able to demonstrate to participants that they were able to follow through on their commitments to PB programs.

However, as PB programs became successful, there was an increase in the number of participants as well as the breadth and cost of the proposed projects, at the same time as the cost of maintaining recently built infrastructure continued to rise. Here is the trap: governments didn't have the revenues and personnel either to implement a greater number of projects or to dramatically increase the value of what could be accomplished. Thus, existing state capacity was sufficiently strong to support a moderate level of small- and medium-sized projects but was unable to support the implementation of greater numbers of more costly projects to keep up with citizens' priorities. Brazil is notorious for having a major deficit of decent housing for its citizens (Donaghy, 2013) and for underfunding elementary and secondary education (Wampler et al., 2020, Chapter 7). These demands are too many and too costly for subnational governments to take on. Although municipal governments do collect property and sales taxes, this doesn't generate enough revenue to address large deficits in public goods provision. Therefore, many cities with PB run up backlogs of projects that are never funded and implemented, which frustrates citizens and makes them lose interest in government-sponsored participation and lose trust in city officials.

The state capacity trap helps to explain why many municipal governments withdrew their early support for municipal-level PB programs. The governments that adopted PB in the context of democratic innovations and civil society renewal were able to make great strides in demonstrating how citizens' voice and vote can be incorporated into government decision-making. They had enough capacity to begin the process of using government resources to produce social and political change, but they lacked the necessary resources to heavily invest in the wider range of public goods that poor residents need in Brazil's urban areas. As we discuss in greater depth in section "What Does This Tell Us About the Greater Spread of PB Across the World?", below, a key lesson is that PB programs might be best situated for middle- (e.g., Brazil, Indonesia, South Africa) and lower-middle-income countries (e.g., Kenya, Philippines). The former programs will more quickly run into the state capacity trap, but the latter countries will take a longer time to fall into the trap because the cost of implementing projects is relatively low. Our worry, discussed below, is that upper-income countries now adopting PB face a different set of problems: they have enough money to work on relatively small projects, but these are not likely to be transformative. Conversely, subnational governments in low-income countries often have very low state capacity, which means that they are unlikely to be able to implement the necessary projects to generate broad support for their programs.

Civil Society

Civil society organizations advocated for adoption of participatory institutions during Brazil's transition to democracy. In terms of democratic innovations, the 1980s in Brazil were a critical juncture, leading to the creation of a wide body of participatory institutions (Pires, 2011; Pogrebinschi & Samuels, 2014; Tranjan, 2016). A generation of civil society activists led the way to devise new institutions and programs that would allow for popular participation and the inclusion of new voices in the political system. Policy councils, which were built out of previous experiences, became the most institutionalized expression of these demands (Almeida et al., 2015; Avritzer, 2009). But PB came to represent the most visible face of these democratic expansion efforts. PB's addition to the democratic cannon was in its ability to mobilize large number of citizens to have them engage in incremental policymaking at the local level.

As PB spread across Brazil, CSOs and social movements engaged with elected governments to mobilize citizens to participate, thus linking civil society and elected governments. Under President Lula, the national government supported yet a third type of state-society engagement, that of the public policy conferences, which had existed in Brazil since the 1940s but on a much smaller scale. The mass mobilization of citizens and CSOs into conferences under Lula led to a shift to a more consultative type of participation. Instead of having citizens directly involved in making "binding decisions" as in PB, citizens were encouraged to participate in institutions that extended them less direct authority and power.

In 2013 and 2014, Brazil was roiled by a series of massive demonstrations. There was a wide range of demands, from better health care to free public transportation to increased transparency. It was telling that there were few broad, systematic demands for more venues for public participation. The institutional structure was in place (the 60,000 policy councils and dozens of policy conferences) but groups advocating for fundamental changes weren't strongly advocating for increasing democratic venues. What explains the shift from 1990 to 2014?

First, the 1980s "democratic innovations" generation of social and political activists was shaped by the military dictatorship (1964–1985). They sought to link the expansion of democracy to the expansion of citizenship rights (Dagnino, 1994, 1998; Holston, 2009). Key members of this generation held political power at state and national levels during the 2000s. Second, civil society in Brazil during the 2000s and 2010 transformed, undergoing a process of "NGOization" (Alvarez, 1999) that left many CSOs functioning as revolving doors between civil society and government. This shift led civil society away from mass participation and mobilization that would have binding authority and to a more policy expert political moment (of course, this coincided with increasing sophistication of Brazil's policy elites). Third, the 2013 and 2014 protests opened the door for conservative social movements to return to the streets. Thematically, these groups advocated for an end to corruption, an increase in transparency, and improvements in service delivery (Saad-Filho, 2013). But demands for increasing citizen participation in policymaking were not central to the overall agenda. In parallel, Brazilian civil society began a process of "evangelization," whereby large marches and demonstrations advocated for a strengthening of traditional family values and the increased role of religion in public life, so much so that McKenna (2020, 167) labels Pentecostals "the most powerful social, political, and cultural movement in Brazil" today. While Brazilian Pentecostals are not unified politically, by the 2010s, the central tendency was not advocating for the expansion of democratic values.

More narrowly, there were distinct trade-offs for the CSOs involved in PB. First, PB is based on routinized participation. There is a standard format of yearly, quarterly, and monthly meetings. It becomes increasingly difficult, over time, for CSOs to mobilize large numbers of participants because these incremental processes increasingly focus on mundane parts of the policymaking process. Quite simply, many PB meetings are a bit boring and dry. It becomes increasingly difficult to sustain mass mobilization when participants are thrust into the bureaucratized world of selecting infrastructure projects.

Second, and directly related to the above issue, there is a disconnect between the lofty claims that PB will be transformative (often asserted by elected officials or the most committed CSOs) and a more limited reality in which PB produces incremental change for a limited number of residents. The projects selected through PB typically affect a single neighborhood or community. These affects can be transformational for the individuals and families living near the project. For example, imagine a community that is connected to the municipal sanitation network; community members no longer have to worry about spilled waste from informal septic tanks that might happen during the rainy season. But these benefits are hard for other people (especially voters) to clearly identify. At the same time, those who benefited from an initial project may view their own continued participation as unnecessary, while those whose projects were not selected may get frustrated and refuse to participate again.

Overall, PB's decline is also associated with the routinization of participation, a distancing of leftist social movements and the rise of conservative and religious groups. The former groups were no longer strongly advocating for an expansion of participatory venues and, for the latter groups, it was never part of their agenda. When citizens and CSOs are interested in participating in policymaking, they will be funneled through the public policy management councils. These incremental institutions have the potential to generate social and political changes, but we should note that they are also heavily bureaucratized bodies that are unlikely to generate strong mobilization.

Deepening the Quality of Democracy

PB began as a radical democratic project, as it founders hoped that these types of participatory institutions would move beyond the confines of actual, existing democracy. PB advocates hoped to use the new process to spark deliberation among citizens so that they better understood their common interests, to expand basic knowledge about budgets and policymaking, to generate a broader discussion about how public revenues are collected and spent, and to alter how and when citizens, CSOs, and governments engage with each other. At the broadest level, several in-depth analyses of PB demonstrate that PB programs have the potential to transform basic state-society relations. The most robust set of findings is presented by Baiocchi et al. (2011), who show that PB increased public participation, changed when and where public deliberation takes place, and altered how governments engage citizens. Their carefully down matched-pair comparison shows how an engaged, politically committed government can invest resources in PB programs to use these programs to promote meaningful change.

Wampler (2008) directly addresses a similar question in an article titled, "When does PB deepen the quality of democracy?" Wampler argues that the deepening of democracy is not a necessary outcome but varies depending on the interactions and interests of governments, CSOs, and citizens. Governments must be willing to delegate real authority and resources to citizens, which places the government in a politically risky position because elected officials are unable to control what occurs within these programs. When governments are able and willing to delegate authority, there is a greater likelihood that PB programs will initiate a basic change in state-society relations. In addition, CSOs and citizens must strike a fine balance in how they participate. They must be willing to partner with government officials, but they must ensure that this partnership doesn't devolve into co-optation, whereby government officials begin to dominate their organizations' political agenda. This balance is often the most difficult for CSOs to achieve because it depends on a combination of partnership and autonomy with an elected government that often has a different set of political and policy goals.

Wampler's analysis of eight cases (2007 and 2008) shows that the deepening of democracy can occur, but it isn't a forgone conclusion. In two of the cases studied, Wampler shows how two PB programs (Porto Alegre and Ipatinga) were contributing to the deepening of democracy, but that in two other cases (Blumenau and Rio Claro) there was little evidence to suggest the deepening of democracy. In four additional cases, the evidence and analysis indicate mixed outcomes. While citizens and CSOs were able to use their voice in public venues and basic citizenship rights were being extended, there was also evidence of co-optation and participatory clientelism.

Our broader analysis in this book also confirms that the duration of many PB program is relatively short—roughly, 50% of PB programs are continued from one mayoral term to the next. Most of those that last longer than 1 term are then in continual existence for 2–3 mayoral terms (8–12 years). This is enough time to begin changing basic state-society relationships. But these programs are hampered by relatively scarce resources (a relatively small percentage of the municipal budget) and municipal-wide participation rates of 4–8% of the population at best. Thus, even if mayors had overcome broader trends in Brazilian political competition, state capacity, and civil society, and had continued to adopt PB at high rates, it is hard to believe that participatory budgeting alone would have been able to generate wide and deep democratic transformation. Furthermore, we unfortunately lack longitudinal studies that could demonstrate if PB programs had a lingering effect even after they were discontinued. In other words, we don't know if there were durable changes in citizens' attitudes and behaviors that continued to be present following PB's discontinuation in most cities. While such changes may be present, researchers have not sought to identify them.

The last years of PB's arc in Brazil (2015–2020) coincide with a profound shift in Brazilian politics. The rush to impeach President Dilma Rousseff in 2015 and 2016 marks a shift away from the emphasis on popular participation, citizenship rights, and the inversion of priorities. Under Presidents Temer and Bolsonaro, the federal government decreased support for popular participation, as evidenced by their eliminating several national policy councils and decreasing support for other councils. These governments also limited the degree of investments in social programs, which made it more difficult for citizens to gain access to basic citizenship rights formally guaranteed during the 1988 Constitutions. These two governments, in addition, advocated for more authoritarian "law and order" practices, which often lead to increased police violence against young men, particularly Afro-Brazilians from poor communities.

Brazil moved across a wide spectrum between 1990 and 2020. The initial period is best characterized as a being a "laboratory of democracy" and the expansion of citizenship rights.

The last several years of this 30-year cycle are characterized by the restriction of participation and citizenship rights. This doesn't mean that Brazil's democracy is in near-term danger of collapsing, but it does mean that some of the key values associated with the 1988 Constitution—such as popular participation and social rights—are being downplayed by the current coalitions in power. We don't necessarily see a political party or a social movement currently assuming a more active role in promoting programs that actively advocate for the direct participation of ordinary citizens in government policymaking. Simply put, there isn't a political actor that appears to be advocating for direct inclusion in PB-like institutions. At the time of this writing (August 2021), political mobilization in Brazil is mostly defensive, with organizing around demands for the impeachment of current president Jair Bolsonaro.

Comparative Lessons

PB is the "participatory institution" of the early twenty-first century (2000–2020) because it combines supply-side and demand-side, bottom-up and top-down, normative (pro-democracy) and technical considerations. Left-leaning civil society and political networks like People Powered and the International Observatory on Participatory Democracy (OIDP) promote PB because it corresponds to their commitment to promote direct citizen engagement. International development organizations like the World Bank and USAID promote it because it addresses key concerns like transparency, good governance, and citizen empowerment. In this section, we return to our analytical framework, emphasizing internal, horizontal, and vertical factors that help to explain PB's adoption, maintenance, and abandonment.

Internal

A clear lesson is that PB fits within the general framework of "All Politics is Local." Our analysis dovetails with other studies of local social accountability and participatory institutions; specifically, the local contexts, by which we mean social, political, and economic conditions, significantly affect how these institutions function. Our assertion about the importance of local conditions is hardly novel or groundbreaking, but it has a particular significance as the basis for comparative analysis. Although there is a growing body of evidence on the adoption of PB in contexts quite distinct from the pioneering cases of Brazil, this evidence suggests enormous variation in how PB plays out on the ground (Baiocchi & Ganuza, 2017; Dias, 2018; Goldfrank, 2011; Wampler et al., 2021).

Importantly, we find that PB has the potential to be a political institution that redistributes power, resources, and authority. But this can only occur when local governments are willing to engage this institution as an explicitly political institution that transfers at least some decision-making power to city residents, which is more likely to occur when governments use PB to energize a political base to use resources differently. When governments using PB don't have strong political incentives to treat PB as a political institution, it becomes much more likely to develop into a low-intensity policy program (see Baiocchi and Ganuza (2017) for an excellent analysis of PB's transformation into a technical policymaking institution).

Our research highlighted the distinctive contexts in which PB developed in dozens of Brazilian cities. Researchers would do well to assess whether local contexts have a similar set of internal incentives to induce government officials to promote PB as a politicized, democratic policymaking institution. Such incentives—stemming from active community groups, political parties ideologically committed to and competing around participatory democracy, and local state capacity to invest significant resources in relevant projects—will vary not only across countries but also across cities within most (democratic) countries.[1] When these incentives are lacking, PB programs are likely to become more similar to technical policymaking tools at best, and we would expect them to have a much weaker impact (Baiocchi & Ganuza, 2017). If not mandated by the national government, these kinds of weak PB programs are likely to be

[1] In most authoritarian countries, relevant local variation in political parties and civil society is unlikely.

abandoned. By the same token, where at least some of these internal incentives are present, even PB programs that started at the urging of external actors are more likely to develop into meaningful and potentially lasting experiments. We say "potentially" because, as the experience of Brazil suggests, parties, civil society, and state capacity are never fixed in time. For example, even for larger cities in middle-income countries like Brazil, as noted above, the state capacity required for initial success in completing projects and promoting participation may prove insufficient over time as citizen demands build up and costs rise.

Horizontal

We found that progressive and "good government" networks helped diffuse PB across Brazilian cities. Do countries elsewhere have such networks? Where they do, PB is more likely to spread faster and be maintained longer. In some regions, such as Europe, these horizontal networks are transnational, like the OIDP, which spans the European Union, as CSOs and governments seek strategies to overcome apathy and disillusionment with democracy. Where PB is nationally mandated, national networks can help in spreading best practices within PB. While international networks may help get pilot PB projects off the ground, it is the within-country horizontal networks that could be crucial to spreading PB across cities.

Partisan horizontal networks are particularly beneficial. When countries have a political party (or coalition) that advances a project based on the basic principles associated with PB, there is a greater likelihood that PB will spread across a country. In Brazil, the promotion of PB within the Workers' Party, as mayors from different cities interacted with each other, was vital to its success. The most analogous situation we identified is in South Korea where a leftist, progressive political party was associated with PB's expansion (Wampler et al., 2021). If we conceptualize PB as a political institution, we would expect that PB will spread more quickly within a political party when (and if) party officials promote it as part of their project. We believe that it is likely to be a quicker route (in comparison to civil society networks) to spreading PB because government officials develop a better understanding of how PB will affect their governing and electoral strategies.

Based on the spread of PB in Brazil, it is becoming increasingly clear that the presence of government officials in these networks is vital. Although civil society organizations can encourage governments to adopt these programs, the evidence from Brazil suggests that the active participation of interested government officials in these networks is crucial. The lesson is that civil society activists working to promote citizen participation and participatory democracy need to actively incorporate elected officials and civil servants into their activities. This means that workshops, seminars, and learning events need to place government officials' interests and perspectives on the same level as CSOs.

Vertical

We found that national rules around decentralization were significant in making PB more or less attractive and viable, and that strong support for PB from a cohesive, programmatic national party was important for its adoption in Brazil as well. Decentralization matters because mayors need both resources and autonomy consistent with their responsibilities in order to implement a PB process that addresses local needs. Brazil's initial wave of decentralization after the 1988 Constitution went a long way toward providing such resources and autonomy (especially for larger cities), while subsequent recentralizing reforms and then economic crisis reduced municipal autonomy and resources, reducing PB's potential. When PB started, Brazil was an outlier compared to most Latin American countries in terms of its high degree of decentralization (Goldfrank, 2007), but with the new rules on "fiscal responsibility," Brazil has lost the advantages it once held for making PB work even if the municipal share of government spending remains higher there than most other countries in the region (Nickson, 2020). To understand PB's trajectory in contexts beyond Brazil, it is therefore important to examine not only the level of resources provided through decentralization, but the specific rules governing budgetary outlays as well.

Another distinctive feature of Brazil for the adoption of PB was the role of the Workers' Party, which helped diffuse PB not only horizontally through mayor-to-mayor connections but also from the top down. That is, during the 1990s and early 2000s, the national party organization highlighted PB's success in major cities and encouraged its mayors to adopt PB as a key part of the *modo petista de governar*. Yet, once the PT reached the presidency and focused on other electorally motivated policies, any prior pressure placed on its mayors to implement participatory budgeting dissipated, suggesting that the notion of a participatory budgeting "policy bubble" within the party makes sense. In most other countries, a party equivalent to the PT—or to what the PT was in the 1990s—does not exist. That is, there are very few large, successful left parties that consistently emphasize popular participation or participatory democracy. The Broad Front in Uruguay is perhaps the closest analog. Other left parties in Latin America once briefly claimed that mantle—in countries like Bolivia, Ecuador, and Venezuela—simultaneously engaged in anti-democratic practices that stripped local-level participation of its democratic transformative potential.

Nonetheless, PB has been adopted in dozens of countries without the presence of a single major party supporting it. International organizations and networks have played a crucial role in promoting PB throughout much of the globe (Goldfrank, 2012; Peck & Theodore, 2015; Porto de Oliveira, 2017). Debates continue over whether such external promotion of PB affects the quality of the programs, leaving the question of how best to encourage meaningful PB open-ended. Here, understanding the interplay of the internal, horizontal, and vertical fields is vital. While vertical and horizontal forces are of utmost importance in shaping the rate of adoption of PB across cities, the internal context is most significant for the quality of PB.

What Does This Tell Us About the Greater Spread of PB Across the World?

PB programs in Brazil were strongest where an ideologically committed political party aligned with its civil society allies, and they spread most quickly when supported by multiple policy networks. Globally, we would expect that PB programs will continue to be adopted by subnational governments when at least one of these PB advocates is present. Although we would expect that these programs will be most successful when all three are present and strongly supportive, we also note that international organizations such as the World Bank and USAID are key drivers of adoption of PB in the Global South. The current moment (2021) would suggest that PB across the world is still involved in an outward expansion, similar to the 1993–2004 period in Brazil. We expect that the gains in the number of PB programs will be more sustainable because several countries formally institutionalized PB in law[2] and because PB has the backing of

[2] According to the Participatory Budgeting World Atlas website (https://www.pbatlas.net/national-legislation-on-pb.html, accessed July 29, 2021), eight countries now have

international policy networks (OIDP, People Powered, Participatory Budgeting Project) as well as multi- and bi-lateral development organizations (World Bank, USAID, DFDD). Thus, we anticipate that PB will continue to spread across the globe. In this final section, we share our concerns that practitioners, citizens, and researchers should consider as they move forward; it is quite possible that we will see an eventual backlash. Governments and international organizations will be disinclined to continue supporting PB if it isn't paying electoral and governance dividends. But, in the final part of this concluding chapter, we also highlight the positive aspects of PB that suggest it will continue to spread and be adopted.

Our first concern is that underlying political conditions in other countries will not support the degree of experimentation and innovation that were present when PB was initially created in Brazil. Simply put, PB was born in a moment of democratic renewal in Brazil. The underlying conditions that promote experimentation are not often present in other countries. Our principal worry is that the uniqueness of Brazil's democratic renewal led to PB's creation and the high functioning programs. We see few other cases with a similar story; the closest might be South Korea and Uruguay. We see the possibility that new social movements (e.g., Black Lives Matter in the US; *Podemos* in Spain) may incorporate similar ideas. It is noteworthy that South Africa, which experienced a different type of democratic renewal in the 1990s, made little progress on strengthening citizen participatory institutions (Heller, 2019). Thus, our principal concern is that Brazil's unique political and social history is quite different than the political histories of many, if not most, other democratizing countries. This suggests the need to insist on more nuance in our analysis of how transitions to democracy in different countries affected the ways in which participatory and direct forms of democracy would be incorporated into the broader institutional structure of representative democracy. Brazil provided fertile ground for a new type of democratic politics. In contrast, other countries didn't have the reconfiguration of civil society and party systems that occurred in Brazil, thus making local leaders much less willing to invest their time and energy into radical democratic experiments.

national laws mandating that subnational governments use PB: Angola, Colombia, Dominican Republic, Ecuador, Indonesia, Panama, Poland, and South Korea. It should be kept in mind, however, that for most of these countries, there are no sanctions for failure to comply, such that on the ground implementation of PB is uneven.

Crucially, Brazil's PB programs made an impact, to a large degree, because most of the implementing governments sought not only to reorganize state-society relations and transform how democracy worked in their cities, but also to build political support. When PB is a highly politicized institution, as it largely was in Brazil, we would expect that it would have a greater short-term impact; at the same time, it is much more likely to be vulnerable to abandonment by subsequent governments. Conversely, we expect PB programs that are more technical or formally institutionalized (but substantively limited) to be more likely to remain in place when elected governments come and go.

Second, we are uncertain if and how PB may guard against democratic backsliding. Theoretically, we can see how this institution may motivate governments to promote democratic values as well as generate more positive associations with democracy among citizens. In other words, PB has the clear potential to expand democratic values and practices. However, we really don't know if supporting PB would be more beneficial than investing in other types of participatory institutions (e.g., public policy management conferences) or in supporting other types of reform efforts focused on classic representative institutions. For example, would it be more beneficial to support campaign finance measures to decrease the illegal use of private resources in election campaigns? Our uncertainty about the potential role of PB guarding against democratic backsliding is thus both theoretical and empirical. Theoretically, we just don't know if PB programs are better (or worse) situated to help stem against backsliding than other democratic reform projects. To the best of our knowledge, we are unaware of any theoretical work that seeks to demonstrate the relative value of different reform projects. Empirically, there is little-to-no research that compares PB to other types of reform programs to assess the degree to which they are producing political outcomes.

Our third uncertainty regarding the expansion of PB is that civil society mobilization is hard to maintain. Brazilian municipalities that adopted PB for more than one term appear to have been able to maintain heightened civil society mobilization for 8–10 years, maybe even 12–14 years, but there is a slow diminishing of mobilization. It is our expectation that other cities and states with PB will experience a similar arc: participation will start slowly, then accelerate, but will then taper off for a variety of reasons. Mobilization cycles are relatively well-established in the academic literature on social movements (Tarrow, 1998), and mobilization in PB programs is not immune to this life cycle. A classic reason why civil society de-mobilization occurs is that it is hard for social movements to sustain the energy and enthusiasm to overcome basic collective action problems. PB, we think, falls into this classic social movement trap because these programs rely on incremental policymaking. It becomes harder and harder to sustain high levels of mass mobilization for incremental, routinized, bureaucratized processes.

A fourth concern is that pro-democracy movements may re-allocate their time and effort to support other types of reform efforts. For example, these movements may focus their attention on promoting greater limits on presidential power or they may seek to show how the judicialization of politics is hampering the protection of basic democratic rights (Avritzer, 2019). The broader point that we want to make is that social movements and community organizations may turn their attention to issues beyond city-level budgetary processes. We note that some municipal governments have sought to transform PB principles to be more supportive of environmental sustainability efforts, yet there hasn't been a systematic analysis of how these relatively small-scale programs may affect broader, deeper issues of climate change.

A fifth concern is that PB is being implemented in authoritarian contexts, such as Russia and China (Cabannes, 2018), helping to lend an aura of legitimacy to governments that use repressive tactics to maintain social and political control. In the most optimistic reading of these programs, PB is being used to create the basic foundations of accountability by creating new forms of state-society relationships. Citizens are allowed to express their policy preferences in public venues, thus showing government officials their basic needs. However, the absence of basic political rights and the basic limitations on free speech make it difficult to know if citizens and community leaders are able to express their core preferences in these environments. Quite simply, we lack evidence and analysis to know if PB is helping to serve as an instrument through which citizens' voice and vote can generate accountability. It is entirely plausible that PB programs in such environments are helping to legitimize authoritarian governments rather than contributing to democracy-enhancing efforts. We recognize that having PB serve to enhance democracy may not be a goal of these PB programs. After all, it is feasible and even likely that technocratic authoritarian rule may be the goal among leaders in Russia and China. However, we would argue that this would subvert the original intent of PB programs, which was to give citizens access to real political power and resources to help change their new democracy. We have seen no evidence on Russia and Chinese programs to suggest that PB is helping to initiate pro-democracy reforms; our worry is that PB is helping to legitimize authoritarian regimes.

A sixth concern is that governments with minimal state capacity won't really be able to implement projects, thereby increasing cynicism about government and democracy. Relatively strong state capacity was a feature that we now recognize as being important to PB's success. It was at a relative sweet spot—enough capacity to get basic projects done, but working in an environment in which relatively small projects could have a meaningful impact. In contrast, we worry that most countries in Sub-Saharan Africa and Southeast Asia will not have sufficient state capacity to implement projects selected by citizens. At the other extreme, we worry that the wealthiest countries (e.g., OCED members) will be unable or unwilling to dedicate the level of resources that is necessary to generate meaningful change.

A final concern is that most new PB programs don't have explicitly pro-poor rules, which limits potential impact. These PB programs have a greater risk of becoming technical tools (Baiocchi & Ganuza, 2017) rather than contributing to radical democratic transformation. When PB programs provide fewer incentives for poor residents to participate, one obviously likely effect is that fewer of them will participate. PB then becomes a program that is more likely to be dominated by middle-class residents who seek to use resources to help their own communities, which only furthers the very inequality that PB was initially meant to redress (Grillos, 2017).

Expansion Signs

Notwithstanding our concerns in the previous section, we see numerous signs that would suggest that PB will continue to spread across the globe. First, some governments, CSOs, and international organizations continue to support democratic innovations. We expect that PB will be transformed as local leaders modify it to address local needs. For example, in cities in the Global North, such as New York City, Chicago, Barcelona, and Taoyuan City (Taiwan), PB programs sought to incorporate immigrants to provide an avenue to formally incorporate these groups into local political institutions (Su, 2016, 2017). In other places, Paris and Madrid most notably, government officials implemented "Digital PB" programs in which most participation occurred online. There are certainly trade-offs with this type of model (e.g., a much thinner version of participation), but we want to highlight that government officials are working within the general spirit of PB (direct citizen engagement on public resources) and creating new ways to engage citizens.

Second, we expect progressive organizations (e.g., Participatory Budgeting Project, People Powered, and OIDP) will continue to support PB because the program principles are well-aligned with the international left. PB is appealing to many on the political left because it promotes the mass mobilization of historically marginalized peoples into public venues to deliberate over government budget priorities. Newly elected leftist governments are often open to adopting PB because it allows them to channel their political base into government policymaking processes. In many ways, PB is an ideal democratic institution for a newly elected leftist government—they are new to power, so it is unclear how they can use state authority and resources to accomplish their political goals. By adopting PB, they can generate support among their followers and legitimize a shift in government spending. Thus, we think that PB will remain popular because it combines mass mobilization with technical decision-making.

Major international organizations, too, support the promotion of PB because it helps them address two inter-related concerns: citizen empowerment and governance. Citizen empowerment has been at the fore of social and political development for much of the past 30 years (Fox, 2015; Mansuri & Rao, 2012; Shah, 2007). International organizations attempt to use PB as a means to generate new attitudes, knowledge, and behaviors among activists as well as to help ensure transparent use of donor funds. In addition, the emphasis on reforming policymaking institutions permits international organizations to provide technical assistance to local government officials.

A third reason why we expect PB to continue to expand across the globe is that many of these programs are positively evaluated by researchers. As Chap. 5 detailed, the vast majority of single-case studies identify positive ways in which PB affects outcomes. Researchers using medium-N, paired-case comparisons, and large-N analyses also identified a series of positive outcomes. When we consider the broader field, it is interesting to note that the general thrust of medium and large-N research confirms many of the insights and findings of the single case studies. An important implication from this work is that it is better for governments to adopt PB than not to adopt PB. In other words, having PB was better than not having it. Within PB programs, it also appears that those governments that used institutional rules more similar to the original PB cases (e.g., use of social justice rules) were more likely to generate more positive PB outcomes.

Although many of the empirical studies identify positive results, caution is merited because many of the positive results are fairly limited in scope. Yes, there is positive change, but it is not radical, fundamental change that would transform society. Rather, PB, even at its most dynamic, is an incremental policymaking process in which change will be at the margins. PB brings a series of positive governance, well-being, and democratic changes that may form the foundations for achieving deeper and more far-reaching change but does not fundamentally shift local social or political structures on its own. We anticipate that PB will continue to spread globally because the allure of combining massive mobilization, public deliberation, and incremental policymaking appeals to governments and civil society allies. Nonetheless, the experience of Brazil's PB programs suggests that many of these programs will have a shelf life of 10–15 years; governments and CSO are likely to slowly withdraw their support when the programs do not produce the radical transformations many of them expected.

References

Abers, R. (2000). *Inventing Local Democracy: Grassroots Politics in Brazil.* Lynne Rienner.

Almeida, C., Cayres, D., & Tatagiba, L. (2015). Balanço dos estudos sobre os conselhos de políticas públicas na última década. *Lua Nova: Revista de Cultura e Política, 94*, 255–294.

Alvarez, S. (1999). Advocating Feminism: The Latin American Feminist NGO 'Boom'. *International Feminist Journal of Politics, 1*(2), 181–209.

Avritzer, L. (2002). *Democracy and the Public Space in Latin America.* Princeton University Press.

Avritzer, L. (2009). *Participatory Institutions in Democratic Brazil.* Woodrow Wilson Center.

Avritzer, L. (2019). *O pêndulo da democracia.* Todavia.

Baiocchi, G. (2005). *Militants and Citizens: The Politics of Participatory Democracy in Porto Alegre.* Stanford University Press.

Baiocchi, G., & Ganuza, E. (2017). *Popular Democracy: The Paradox of Participation.* Stanford University Press.

Baiocchi, G., Heller, P., & Silva, S. (2011). *Bootstrapping Democracy: Transforming Local Governance and Civil Society in Brazil.* Stanford University Press.

Cabannes, Y. (2018). Highlights on Some Asian and Russian Participatory Budgeting Pioneers. In N. Dias (Ed.), *Hope for Democracy: 30 Years of Participatory Budgeting Worldwide* (pp. 235–254). Oficina.

Dagnino, E. (1994). *Os Anos 90: Politica e Sociedade no Brasil.* Editora Brasiliense.

Dagnino, E. (1998). The Cultural Politics of Citizenship, Democracy and the State. In S. Alvarez, S. E. Dagnino, & A. Escobar (Eds.), *Cultures of Politics/ Politics of Cultures: Re-visioning Latin American Social Movements.* Westview Press.

Dias, N. (2018). *Hope for Democracy: 30 Years of Participatory Budgeting Worldwide.* Epopeia Records and Oficina.

Donaghy, M. M. (2013). *Civil Society and Participatory Governance: Municipal Councils and Social Housing Programs in Brazil.* Routledge.

Faria, C. F. (2003). Do conflito jurídico ao consenso: uma versão da implementaçãodo OP-RS. In L. Avritzer & Z. Navarro (Eds.), *A inovação democratica no Brasil: o orçamento participativo* (pp. 240–272). Cortez.

Fedozzi, L. (1997). *Orçamento Participativo: Reflexões Sobre a Experiência de Porto Alegre.* Tomo Editorial.

Fox, J. (2015). Social Accountability: What Does the Evidence Really Say? *World Development, 72*, 346–371.

Fung, A., & Wright, E. O. (Eds.). (2003). *Deepening Democracy: Institutional Innovations in Empowered Participatory Governance.* Verso.

Goldfrank, B. (2007). Lessons from Latin American Experience in Participatory Budgeting. In A. Shah (Ed.), *Participatory Budgeting.* World Bank Institute.

Goldfrank, B. (2011). *Deepening Local Democracy in Latin America: Participation, Decentralization, and the Left.* Pennsylvania State University Press.

Goldfrank, B. (2012). The World Bank and the Globalization of Participatory Budgeting. *Journal of Public Deliberation, 8*(2), 7.

Goldfrank, B. (2017). Participatory Budgeting in Latin American Cities. In T. Angotti (Ed.), *Urban Latin America: Inequalities and Neoliberal Reforms.* Rowman & Littlefield.

Gonçalves, S. (2014). The Effects of Participatory Budgeting on Municipal Expenditures and Infant Mortality in Brazil. *World Development, 53*, 94–110.

Grillos, T. (2017). Participatory Budgeting and the Poor: Tracing Bias in a Multi-Staged Process in Solo, Indonesia. *World Development, 96*, 343–358.

Heller, P. (2019). Divergent Trajectories of Democratic Deepening: Comparing Brazil, India, and South Africa. *Theory and Society, 48*(3), 351–382.

Holston, J. (2009). *Insurgent Citizenship: Disjunctions of Democracy and Modernity in Brazil.* Princeton University Press.

Hunter, W. (2010). *The Transformation of the Workers' Party in Brazil, 1989–2009.* Cambridge University Press.

Mansuri, G., & Rao, V. (2012). *Localizing Development: Does Participation Work?* The World Bank.

Marquetti, A. (2003). Democracia, Equidade e Effciencia, o Caso do Orçamento Participativo em Porto Alegre. In L. Avritzer & Z. Navarro (Eds.), *A Inovação Democrática no Brasil: O Orçamento Participativo* (pp. 129–156). Cortez Editores.

McKenna, E. (2020). *The Revolution Will Be Organized: Power and Protest in Brazil's New Republic, 1988-2018* (Ph.D. Dissertation). University of California, Berkeley.

Nickson, A. (2020). Local Government in Latin America: The Struggle to Overcome Social Exclusion. In R. Kerley, J. Liddle, & P. Dunning (Eds.), *The Routledge Handbook of International Local Government* (pp. 131–148). Routledge.

Peck, J., & Theodore, N. (2015). *Fast Policy: Experimental Statecraft at the Thresholds of Neoliberalism*. University of Minnesota Press.

Pires, R. (2011). *Efetividade das instituições participativas no Brasil: estratégias de avaliação*. IPEA.

Pogrebinschi, T., & Samuels, D. (2014). The Impact of Participatory Democracy: Evidence from Brazil's National Public Policy Conferences. *Comparative Politics, 46*(3), 313–332.

Porto de Oliveira, O. (2017). *International Policy Diffusion and Participatory Budgeting: Ambassadors of Participation, International Institutions and Transnational Networks*. Palgrave Macmillan.

Saad-Filho, A. (2013). Mass Protests Under 'Left Neoliberalism': Brazil, June-July 2013. *Critical Sociology, 39*(5), 657–669.

Samuels, D., & Zucco, C. (2018). *Partisans, Antipartisans, and Nonpartisans: Voting Behavior in Brazil*. Cambridge University Press.

Santos, B. (Ed.). (2005). *Democratizing Democracy: Beyond the Liberal Democratic Canon*. Verso.

Shah, A. (2007). *Participatory Budgeting*. World Bank.

Su, C. (2016). *Re-Engaging the Disenfranchised: Participatory Budgeting in the United States*. Brookings Institution Press.

Su, C. (2017). Beyond Inclusion: Critical Race Theory and Participatory Budgeting. *New Political Science, 39*(1), 126–142.

Tarrow, S. (1998). *Power in Movement: Social Movements and Contentious Politics* (2nd ed.). Cambridge University Press.

Touchton, M., & Wampler, B. (2014). Improving Social Well-Being Through New Democratic Institutions. *Comparative Political Studies, 47*(10), 1442–1469.

Tranjan, R. (2016). *Participatory Democracy in Brazil: Socioeconomic and Political Origins*. University of Notre Dame Press.

Wampler, B. (2007). *Participatory Budgeting in Brazil: Contestation, Cooperation, and Accountability*. Pennsylvania State University Press.

Wampler, B. (2008). When Does Participatory Democracy Deepen the Quality of Democracy? Lessons from Brazil. *Comparative Politics, 41*(1), 61–81.
Wampler, B., Sugiyama, N. B., & Touchton, M. (2020). *Democracy at Work: Pathways to Well-Being in Brazil.* Cambridge University Press.
Wampler, B., McNulty, S., & Touchton, M. (2021). *Participatory Budgeting in Global Perspective.* Oxford University Press.
Wampler, B., & Touchton, M. (2019). Designing Institutions to Improve Social Well-Being: Evidence from Across Brazil's Participatory Budgeting Programs. *European Journal of Political Research, 58*(3), 915–937.

The manufacturer's authorised representative in the EU is Springer Nature Customer Service Centre GmbH, Europaplatz 3, 69115 Heidelberg, Germany. If you have any concerns regarding our products, please contact ProductSafety@springernature.com

Printed and bound by CPI Group (UK) Ltd, Croydon, CR0 4YY
30/09/2026
02225472-0006